Living on Love

Living on Love

Cooking When You're Short
On Time and Cash

Annie Oeth

Mojo Triangle Books™
an imprint of

SARTORIS
LITERARY
GROUP

A traditional publisher
with a non-traditional approach to publishing

SARTORIS LITERARY GROUP, INC.
Metro-Jackson, Mississippi
www.sartorisliterary.com

For those who pull up a chair at our table. Be blessed!

CONTENTS

Living on Love

Photo credit: © Melanie Thortis

Foreword

"What are you living on … love?"

As a former picky child, I used to hear that a lot. Because I sure wasn't living on turnip greens. Those are an acquired taste, and one that I didn't care to acquire as a nine-year-old.

The meaning of this old expression, living on love, is that you're not eating enough. Love's apparently all you're taking in. This wasn't said in a pleasant tone, either. More like exasperated. Picky children are loved dearly, but their finicky behavior isn't always liked.

Eventually, I outgrew my suspicions about green vegetables, onions and casseroles, but I never lost my ability to live on love.

After all, you can live without turnip greens, but you can't live without love.

We show love in all kinds of ways, and one of the most obvious and delicious ways is in the kitchen. Men grill. Grandmothers bake. Moms serve up pot roasts and fried chicken. Like the old commercial said, "Nothing says lovin' like something from the oven."

My Gentleman Friend has cooked my dinner quite a few times and has gifted me with hand-dipped chocolate-covered strawberries that were dipped by his hands. He's pretty smart, that man, because I am a total chow hound. The path to my heart may not run straight through my stomach, but you can see it from there.

Delving into religion, I don't think it's by accident that quite a few of Jesus' miracles included food, whether it was feeding 5,000 people with the donation of a boy's fish and bread or showing up after the resurrection at the shore cooking fish. If Jesus was Southern, he'd have been serving up catfish and hushpuppies at a fish fry.

His first public miracle involved wine at a wedding celebration.

Coincidence? I think not.

If you want to show love, if you want to connect with someone, feed them. Or let them serve something up for you. There are few things as personal or as pleasurable as cooking and sharing a meal.

Once I was talking with a coworker, a young man who ran the press at the newspaper where I was working at the time. He was in love.

How did I know? Because he was telling us all, the lunch bunch in the break room, about the dinner his girlfriend made him. He went into great detail about how wonderful the meal was. The entrée was Hamburger Helper. The kind with the Helping Hand on the front of the box. I'm not going to pretend I haven't eaten my share of Hamburger Helper, but this young man was waxing eloquent over the beef stroganoff flavor.

Was it really that good? I doubt it. Any of us in the break room could have whipped up a batch of Hamburger Helper, and it would have been your garden variety boxed dinner mix.

But in the hands of his beloved, it was to rival

anything whipped up by Martha Stewart or her minions. It doesn't matter as much what's served as who's doing the serving. Hamburger Helper served with love is an enviable dish indeed.

On Labor Day 2014, I had talked my oldest Dear Son into doing the grilling of hamburgers for our family feast.

"So were you working today?" he asked.

"No, I'm off," I said.

"But I didn't see you this morning."

I told him I was using the day off from my editing gig at *The Clarion-Ledger* to write this, my third book, a recipe collection.

"You're writing a cookbook?" he laughed. "Who'd want to cook like *you*? You talked *me* into cooking today!"

He may view that as a lack of cooking skills.

I call it genius.

I would be willing to venture that quite a few would like to cook like I do if my cooking involved delegating the meal preparation to somebody else.

When it comes to dinners, and especially those grilled, I can be the Tom Sawyer of the house, telling my children and the Gentleman Friend how wonderfully they grill and how good their chicken and burgers and salmon are.

It's not hollow praise, either. They all are fantastic in the kitchen and at the grill. Even the youngest, the Dear Daughter, makes a mean batch of chicken fried rice.

A dinner that you didn't have to cook is more delicious.

Even better than that is one served up by your children, because you know they won't starve when they're on their own, and by your significant other, because cooking is a way of showing love and affection. I'd take a dinner cooked at home over roses any day.

You can live on love and grilled chicken and dinners that you may or may not have cooked yourself.

It doesn't get much better than that.

—**Annie Oeth**

1

Tips, Tricks and Secret Weapons, Plus a Little Philosophy

First Things First

This analogy has been told and retold. If you're on an airplane, and the oxygen masks fall down, you put yours on first. Then you help others put on their masks.

You take care of yourself first. Because otherwise you will pass out from lack of oxygen.

That's a great metaphor for cooking, because if you don't take care of yourself, the cook, for crying out loud, you will pass out. Or feel like passing out. Or curse out a close friend or someone you either married or gave birth to.

First things first, and you come first.

Before you set the oven to 350 or so much as open the refrigerator, you have to set the stage for a happy cook and not a scene of domestic strife or burned pork chops.

Here are some tips. Follow them to be happier and not yell at the children or animals who live in your house.

• **Be comfortable**. I can't stress this enough. I may have on a pencil skirt and my power pumps when I hit the door at the end of the day with a couple of bags of groceries in my arms, but I don't need to stay that way. Stay that way, and the high heels will make me say ugly things. Jeans, a T-shirt and tennis shoes are my comfy clothes. A comfy cook is a happy cook.

• **Be happy**. I used to try to make complicated dishes and the food might have been good, but I was also fussing at those near and dear. Nothing tastes good enough to cover crankiness. If you don't enjoy making it or eating it, then what are you doing?

- **Make things your crew likes to eat**. I have made the misstep of cooking something I found in a foodie magazine only to find that nobody liked it.

- **Make your family's favorites**—they'll love you for it, and the food will disappear. If no one eats the recipe, then you're wasting time and money.

- **Who said you had to make everything and do everything yourself?** Restaurants, delis and supermarkets make pasta, casseroles, breads and sides to go, and there are already prepped and bagged salads available at your nearest produce section. The time you save can be time spent relaxing after a long day or, better yet, having fun with the people you love. Serve up the store-bought goodies in your own serving dishes if it makes you feel better.

- **Take shortcuts**. Some things, such as aluminum foil for lining pans and nonstick cooking spray for ease in serving and less stressful clean-up later on, help me keep my sanity. Ditto for ready-made pie crusts, because while I am capable of making a pie crust, it's not something I want to do or enjoy doing. Make the things you enjoy making and take shortcuts on the rest.

- **If you're entertaining, just because you are hosting doesn't mean you have to do the cooking, too**. Ask your guests to bring sides, appetizers or desserts, and your family can do the grilling or serve up the lasagna. It's more fun that way, as your guests will enjoy showing off their cooking skills and you'll enjoy your company.

• **Start clean**. Yeah, I know, some people don't like to clean. Actually, I don't mind doing dishes, and if you do the cooking, I'll gladly clean up. Dish soap smells like everything from lemons to a tropical vacation. If you start with a clean sink with your dirty dishes in the dishwasher, I promise you, you will feel more relaxed and have more room.

• **Clean as you go**. Really? More cleaning? Yes. Because if you get into the habit of cleaning as you go, rinsing and putting dirty pots, pans, bowls and spoons into the dishwasher, you won't have a stack piled up in the sink just when you want to relax after dinner.

• **Start early**. Got a few minutes after dinner the night before? Or in the morning? Use it to get a head start on dinner for the next evening. And this requires …

• **A plan**. This is always a hard thing for me, but if you have one of these things called a "plan," then you can have your ingredients on hand and get a head start on prep work. Chop your onions, make your lemon ice box pie, or at least have some sort of a game plan.

• **Start dinner**. Preheat the oven, start sautéing veggies, browning ground beef or tossing salad. Do what you have to do.

• **Drink wine**. Or iced tea. Whatever you like. Start pouring the second after you start the oven but before you chop onions, because wine helps you ignore how odious onion-chopping can be.

- **Sit at the table**. I am not going to pretend we do this every night or even most nights. However, eating at the table away from electronics is a good thing. Make a big deal out of it – put the bread in a cloth-lined basket, set the table with some nice china and enjoy the blessings God put in your life.

Only Mama Cooks Like Mama

Years ago, as a young wife, I wanted to do the impossible. That would be cooking like my late husband, Baby Daddy's mama.

Let's stop right here and hand out some advice. Men, never tell your wives or girlfriends you wish they cooked like your mothers. Think it if you have to, but those words never need to leave your mouth.

Brag on their cooking, not your mother's. And if your better half burns everything that hits a pan, then, as my Aunt Tootsie used to say, if you can't say anything nice, don't say anything at all.

For the love of all that is holy, never tell the love of your life that you wished she cooked like your mother.

Rather than inform Baby Daddy that I was not his mother, I tried the impossible. There were two things he missed from his boyhood: Hamburger Green Bean Bake and Hershey Bar Pie. I tried to make both. I even had his mother's recipes.

There are a couple of reasons why this didn't work. One was that recipes from decades prior may or may not translate in today's kitchens.

Sizes of Hershey Bars change, for example. Some products are no longer made. Groceries change, just like hair styles and hemlines.

But here is the main reason that you can't cook like his mother.

No wife or girlfriend can ever cook like mama because they are not mama.

No two people ever cook the same way. If you handed out the same recipe to a roomful of people, you would have fifty different versions. Each one would be a little bit different.

The onions would be diced in different sizes. Some would be seasoned more than others. There are people who follow a recipe to the letter and never vary from what's written down, and there are people like me who consider recipe instructions to be "suggestions." We substitute and add and decide, "Oh, what the heck, I'm putting a whole green pepper in."

Call it an affirmation that God did indeed make each of us unique. Like a fingerprint, our cooking styles are ours alone.

Men who tell their wives that they can't cook like their mothers are destined to be lonely. They need to ask themselves whether they want to say what's on their minds or be happily married.

It got worse, though. I said that, one day, our sons' wives would not cook like me, and the suggestion was made that, oh, yes, they could.

They could order pizza just like I do.

Men, this is another one of those thoughts that needs to never leave your head.

Was Baby Daddy telling the truth? Sure, he was.

Truth-telling never made a good marriage, though. Never say "yes" if your spouse asks if something makes her look fat, and never tell the truth about cooking unless the food's fabulous.

There were times in my marriage that I hung in there because I love Jesus, and after being told that was one of those times.

Like lying, forgiveness is a big part of being happily married.

So anyhow, cooking like anyone else but you is impossible. If you used recipes by Martha Stewart, you'd be putting your spin, your flavor, on Martha's "suggestions."

With this in mind, here are my recipes.

Put your own spin on them.

Hamburger Green Bean Bake

Cost $8
Prep 30 minutes / Bake Time 30 minutes

1 pound ground beef
1 medium-sized onion, chopped
1 can tomato soup
Salt and pepper
1 can cut green beans, drained
3-5 medium-sized potatoes, more or less depending
   on the size of your family
Milk
Butter
Shredded cheese blend (optional)

Peel potatoes and boil. Brown ground beef and chopped onion until done and drain. Return meat and onion to skillet and add can of tomato soup, adding salt and pepper to taste. Add water if needed for consistency.

Preheat oven to 350. Spray your favorite casserole dish with nonstick cooking spray. Put meat mixture in casserole. Top that layer with canned green beans.

Drain potatoes, and with electric mixer, beat with amount of milk and butter needed for a batch of Whooped Taters. Season with salt and pepper or Cajun seasoning to taste. Spoon mashed potatoes over top of green beans. Top with pats of butter or sprinkle with shredded cheese if desired.

Bake for about 30 minutes or until potatoes are browned slightly and casserole is heated through.

Hershey Bar Pie
Cost $4
Prep Time 30 minutes

1 baked 9-inch pie crust, cooled
1 7-ounce Hershey chocolate bar, broken into pieces
1/3 cup milk
1 ½ cups miniature marshmallows or 15 large
   marshmallows
1 cup cold whipping cream

In top of a double boiler, melt broken chocolate bar with milk, stirring frequently. Add marshmallows, stirring until melted. Remove from top of boiling water and cool to room temperature.

In small bowl, beat whipping cream until stiff and fold into chocolate mixture. Or do like I did and just use the whipped topping in a tub. (Remember what I said about thinking of recipes as "suggestions?")

Spoon this into your cooled pie crust and refrigerate until pie is firm. Garnish with whipped cream, or in my case, whipped topping.

Being Friends With Your Food

I've never been one to count calories.

For one thing, counting calories involves math, maybe even algebra. Math and I have never gotten along.

But more importantly, keeping track of every morsel of food that passes your lips just sucks all the joy out of eating. Not only that, but it has you thinking about what you can't have. All. The. Time.

At least, that is how my mind works.

Years ago, I had one of those Richard Simmons Deal-A-Meal card sets. You'd get so many cards with food items and amounts on them, and as you ate the food on the cards, you move the cards from one side of the wallet to the other. When you run out of cards, you are done eating.

Or so the theory goes.

I ran out of cards ridiculously early and was that lovely combination of hungry and angry, or hangry, the rest of the day. My family was telling me I didn't need to lose an ounce just so I would stop with the diet cards and be a nice person again.

When I was playing cards with my diet, I really wasn't enjoying food. I was obsessing on it.

Now there are fitness bracelets with GPS step counters. My oldest Dear Son bought me one for Christmas. Those will let you record what you eat through an app on your cell phone, and then, as you move around during the day, it does the math of what you ate vs. how many calories you burned.

I had some lemon icebox pie at a church supper one Wednesday night and started walking around the block with the dog until I had burned off my pie calories.

It was a little better than the cards, since with the fitness bracelet, I can earn food through walking around. I love food, so I will gladly walk for pie.

Still, using the pedometer fitness bracelet still requires the counting of calories. And math. And honesty.

Generally, I am an honest person, but I will lie to my FitBit.

Here is what works for me, and while I am not a size 2, I am healthy and not hangry most of the time.

Make friends with your food. Stop calling some foods "bad." Realize that food is there for your pleasure and nourishment. Enjoy it, for crying out loud.

This does not mean sitting on the sofa and eating a whole box of Ding-Dongs, though.

You have to make some smart choices. Sometimes, when I make tacos for the kids, I have a big taco salad and skip the tortillas or at least some of them. It's yummy, big, spicy and I am not feeling deprived.

I'll also have pizza with the kids, but I have one piece with a big salad on the side. Also a glass of red wine. Because the doctor says I should drink a glass of red wine. This is true only if I nickname myself "the doctor," but I feel like I am enjoying a meal instead of living on starvation rations.

I love Brussels sprouts, steamed with lemon juice and butter. One of the most recent times I enjoyed this veggie, made only for me since the rest of the family are not sprouts fans, I served it with a more family-friendly Meat Loaf and Whooped Taters. I enjoyed a deck of cards-sized piece of Meat Loaf and somewhere around a half cup to two-thirds cup of Whooped Taters, but lots of Brussels sprouts. Unlimited.

Then there are things I do to be a Spartan now and indulge later.

I'm not much of a gym goer. I like to move around outside instead. So I will make sure to go for a nice run or a long walk with friends if I am planning on going out for wings, brews and football-watching later.

Then there are the theories that some activities can actually cancel out calories. A diet soda with dessert evens it all out to zero calories.

Broken cookies are OK to eat since all the calories leak out from the crumbled parts.

Desserts have to be sampled before serving them to others, because you have to make sure they're good. Those calories don't count.

Calories from a dessert eaten with a friend don't count because you are eating dessert out of friendship. Friends don't let friends eat dessert alone.

Life is a fleeting thing, and it is meant to be enjoyed, like a buffet.

Food is one of life's greatest pleasures, and sharing a delicious meal with those you love is something that should be savored. Enjoy your calories, stop counting them during the fantastic and memorable meals, have a dessert every so often and take a few walks to even things out.

Bon appétit!

2

It's 5 o'clock Somewhere
Recipes for Appetizers,
Tailgating
and the Cocktail Hour

Grazing

People love food. Evidence to this fact is that we enjoy food before we enjoy more food.

Appetizers. Canapes. Crudites. Chips and dip. Fruit and dip. Veggies and dip. Bread and dip. Snack mix.

You name it, and we graze on it.

It is a wonder I don't have multiple stomachs like a bovine because I graze. Be it a benefit fundraiser buffet or a tailgate spread, I hang around the buffet table and nibble away.

We grazers have tricks, though, to make it appear as if we are not eating at all.

For instance, don't get a plate. Then you can pick up one sausage ball, for instance, and once you have gobbled that up, you look like you are exercising all kinds of self control.

There is that famous tip, one I heard in *Gone With The Wind* when Scarlett is being advised to eat before going to a party so she will appear dainty with her small appetite.

This, I believe, is bad advice. The whole point of going to a party, other than seeing your friends, of course, is to eat other people's food. So graze, but not obviously.

If you pick up a tiny quiche, don't walk around with it. Don't say grace over it. Just eat the thing. Then eat some of the tiny quiche's friends, maybe the cocktail meatballs over in the Crock Pot or the Hawaiian bread and spinach dip.

If you are going to get a plate, load that up with baby carrots and celery sticks, strawberries and melon balls. Then you can be healthier than thou visually, and those healthy choices have been scientifically proven to remove calories from Pigs in Blankets and anything from the chocolate fountain.

Some buffet spreads are a coffee-and-tea-type thing, and some you might enjoy with a soda or with one of those punches made with raspberry sherbet and ginger ale. Then there are buffets that accompany happy hour, which can be any old time if you consider that there are drinks such as mimosas and bloody Marys that are not only acceptable at brunch but encouraged, depending on whose buffet you're visiting.

In the latter kind of buffets, since I am a light-weight when it comes to drinking, the cheese spreads, canapés, cocktail meatballs and pigs in blankets are eaten as part of a buzz management plan.

Munch so whatever your poison is doesn't poison you. Or just sip on a soda, iced tea or water. Nobody ever said you had to be throwing back cocktails like there is no tomorrow.

Whatever kind of buffet you're enjoying, mix and mingle, and swap a recipe or two.

Mississippi Sin

Cost $12

Prep Time 30 minutes / Bake Time 45 minutes

This is one bad boy dip, and it is aptly named. I could eat a whole loaf myself and ask for forgiveness later.

2 cups shredded cheddar cheese
1 8-ounce block cream cheese, softened
1 ½ cups sour cream
1/2 cup cooked ham, chopped fine
1 small can green chilies
1/3 cup chopped green onions
1/8 tsp. Worcestershire sauce
1 round loaf French bread

In a medium- to large-sized mixing bowl, combine all ingredients except bread and stir until blended.

With serrated knife, slice a thin piece of bread from top of loaf and set aside. With knife, slice vertically into the loaf, stopping about a half-inch from the bottom of the loaf. Cut around until you have a cylindrical piece of bread at the center that has been cut away.

Remove center of loaf. Cut removed bread into half-inch cubes and set aside.

Fill center of bread with dip, and replace the top slice cut from loaf. Wrap in aluminum foil and bake in a 350-degree oven for about 45 minutes to 1 hour.

Serve with reserved bread cubes, crackers, veggies and other favorite dippers.

John's Favorite Finger Sandwiches
Cost $10
Prep Time 30 minutes / Bake Time 45 minutes

These were whipped up for the middle Dear Son's senior guitar recital at Mississippi State University, meaning they were made at home and traveled a couple of hours, no worse for the wear. A tip, though: To have moist/not dried out finger sandwiches, pack them in layers in a covered plastic container with damp paper towels between the layers.

2 bunches green onions, sliced thinly
1 pound bacon, cooked, drained and crumbled (or use real bacon bits from the salad dressing area of your supermarket)
2 8-ounce packages cream cheese, softened
½ cup mayonnaise, regular or light
1 tsp. Worcestershire sauce

In mixing bowl, stir together all ingredients until well blended. Spread on bread, white or wheat, cutting off crusts.

Spiced Wine
Cost $20
Prep Time 10 minutes / Cook Time 3-4 hours

I made this once for a Tupperware party. Because it is delicious and also because no one buys Tupperware like women drinking wine. This will also make your kitchen smell wonderful.

2 bottles dry red wine
3 oranges, peeled and sliced into wedges (save the peels)
2 Tbsp. whole cloves
½ cup sugar
1 cinnamon stick

Poke cloves into the orange peels and put in the bottom of your Crock Pot. Pour in wine and sugar and drop in the cinnamon stick. Cover and cook on low 3-4 hours.

Cheese Ball
Cost $7
Prep Time 30 minutes

This is a classic recipe, and having a Cheese Ball whipped up and in your refrigerator makes entertaining easy.

2 8-ounce blocks of cream cheese, regular, reduced fat or fat-free
1 jar dried beef or 1 jar real bacon bits
1 bunch green onions, chopped
1 tsp. Worcestershire sauce

Place cream cheese in a large mixing bowl. In food processor, chop dried beef fine, or just skip that step and use a jar of real bacon bits.

Divide meat in half, reserving part in a separate bowl.

Mix cream cheese, half of meat, onions and Worcestershire sauce until blended. Form into a ball, and roll ball in remaining chopped meat or bacon bits.

Refrigerate at least one hour. Serve with your favorite crackers.

Ritzy Cheese Mold
Cost $10
Prep Time 30 minutes

This is a favorite of mine, having just a little sweetness to balance out that sharp cheddar.

2 cups sharp cheddar cheese, shredded
¾ cup mayonnaise
½ cup chopped pecans
Dash hot sauce
½ cup strawberry preserves

Blend together all ingredients except strawberry preserves. This can be done by hand, with mixer or with a food processor. Line a 4-cup ring mold with plastic wrap and fill with cheese mixture. If you don't have a mold, just shape cheese mixture into a ring. Refrigerate for several hours. To serve, place on platter, with strawberry preserves in the center of the ring. Accompany with crackers. This goes especially well with Ritz crackers.

Dog Food Snacks
Cost $10
Prep Time 30 minutes

1 stick butter or margarine
12 ounces chocolate chips
1 cup creamy peanut butter
1 box Crispix cereal
2 cups confectioner's sugar

This is not really dog food, but it's the name given to this addictive snack by Joyce Aycock, who was a circuit clerk at the time she made this recipe and brought it to work. She was sweet enough to share this with me when I was working as a newspaper reporter and was covering a trial in circuit court. The recipe, which has also gone by the name "Muddy Buddies," does look sort of like dog food, but it's for people, not puppies.

Melt butter, chocolate chips and peanut butter in a saucepan on low heat. Pour cereal into a large mixing bowl. Pour butter-chocolate-peanut butter mixture over cereal and stir to coat.

Pour confectioner's sugar into a large plastic bag. Pour cereal into bag and shake.

Meatballs

Cost $8
Prep Time 15 minutes / Bake Time 20-30 minutes

These are yummy and can be made ahead of time, which will make your holiday entertaining easier.

1 pound ground beef
1 tsp. Worcestershire sauce
2/3 cup evaporated milk
1 envelope onion soup mix

Sauce:
1 cup ketchup
½ cup brown sugar
½ Tbsp. Worcestershire

Preheat oven to 350. Mix Worcestershire sauce, ground beef, evaporated milk and onion soup mix until combined.

Form meat into meatballs and place on broiler pan. Bake for about 20-30 minutes or until done.

Mix sauce ingredients and simmer in a saucepan for about 10 minutes. Add meatballs and serve with toothpicks.

John's Guacamole

Cost $5
Prep Time 10 minutes

2 avocados
Salsa (live a little and go with medium or hot)
1 lime
Salt and pepper

One night around the holidays, my middle son, John, came home from college. He and I were enjoying catching up and decided we needed something to munch on. Off to the supermarket we went, and among the items we picked up were some avocados and some tortilla chips. We winged it as far as the guacamole recipe, but it came out pretty nicely.

Cut avocados in half, remove the pits and spoon out avocado into a mixing bowl. Squeeze in fresh lime juice. Season to taste with salt and pepper. Add a little salsa – quicker than chopping tomatoes, onions and peppers. Put into your favorite serving bowl and serve with tortilla chips. Great for eating while sitting up with your children.

Rosemary Roasted Nuts
Cost $15
Prep Time 30 minutes

These are a favorite at our place during the holidays, and this was also served up, with my middle son's favorite nuts, cashews, at the Famous Maroon guitar recital. Plant a little rosemary in your yard and you'll be ready to make this whenever you'd like.

> 1½ pounds nuts – cashews and pecans work
>   especially well
> 2 Tbsp. fresh rosemary leaves, coarsely chopped
> ½-1 tsp. Cajun seasoning, depending on taste
> 2 tsp. brown sugar
> 1 Tbsp. butter, melted (the real thing is delicious
>   in this recipe!)

Preheat oven to 375. In a mixing bowl, combine all ingredients, tossing to coat nuts. Spread nuts on baking sheet and bake for 8-10 minutes, stirring as necessary and watching to prevent nuts from over-browning. When toasty, remove and let nuts cool on baking sheet. Store in covered plastic container.

Seven-layer Mexican Dip

Cost $15
Prep Time 30 minutes

1 envelope taco seasoning
1 can refried beans
1 8-ounce block of cream cheese
2 cups sour cream
1 jar salsa, hot or mild
1 tomato, chopped
1 green pepper, chopped
1 bunch green onions, chopped
1 small head iceberg lettuce, sliced thin or shredded
1 can sliced black olives
2 cups cheddar cheese, shredded

I have friends who just can't watch football without this dip. And it is so good I could polish off a whole dish on my own! Serve with your favorite crunchy dippers such as tortilla chips, corn chips or crackers.

In a mixing bowl, blend taco seasoning and refried beans. Spread this in a pie plate or shallow serving dish as your first layer. Blend sour cream and cream cheese. Spread over beans for second layer.

Top this with a layer of salsa for the third layer. Then top that with tomato (fourth layer), green pepper (fifth layer), green onions (sixth layer) and lettuce (seventh layer).

Top this with cheddar cheese and black olives for garnish and dig in.

Chocolate Chip Cheese Ball
Cost $10 or less
Prep Time 30 minutes

The Dear Daughter tried this as a youth volunteer in Vacation Bible School and loved it so much she got the recipe for me! It's got all the great addictive flavors of chocolate chip cookie dough, so what's not to love?

1 8-ounce block of cream cheese, softened
½ cup butter, softened
¾ cup confectioner's sugar
2 Tbsp. brown sugar
¼ tsp. vanilla
¾ cup miniature chocolate chips
¾ cup chopped pecans

In a mixing bowl, beat together cream cheese and butter until smooth. Blend in confectioner's sugar, brown sugar and vanilla. Stir in chocolate chips. Roll mixture into a ball, and roll ball in chopped pecans. Serve with honey graham crackers or chocolate graham crackers.

Football Cheese Ball
Cost $8
Prep Time 30 minutes

1 8-ounce packages cream cheese, softened
1 cup cheddar cheese, shredded
¼ cup green onions, chopped
2 Tbsp. Worcestershire sauce
½ envelope taco seasoning mix
½ slice American cheese, sliced into strips

If you want something for that Super Bowl party or tailgate, this is something showy to bring. And it will disappear in a hurry.

In mixing bowl, blend cream cheese, cheddar cheese, green onions, Worcestershire sauce and taco seasoning until well blended. Shape into a football, and turn out onto piece of plastic wrap.

Place the football-shaped cheese ball onto a serving plate and arrange strips of American cheese on top to resemble laces on a football. Refrigerate for at least two hours, and take out of refrigerator about 30 minutes before serving to allow cheese to soften.

Surround with your favorite crackers.

Baked Buffalo Wings

Cost $10
Prep Time 30 minutes

¾ cup all-purpose flour
½ tsp. cayenne pepper
½ tsp. garlic powder
1/2 -1 tsp. salt
20 chicken wings
½ cup melted butter
½ cup hot wing sauce (Frank's is a good one!)

One of my favorite things to do in the fall is go out for Buffalo chicken wings and cold beer and watch football with friends. Here's something to whip up if you decide to stay home to watch the big game.

Preheat oven to 400. Line a baking sheet with aluminum foil and spray it with nonstick cooking spray. In a gallon-sized zippered plastic bag, mix flour, cayenne pepper, garlic powder and salt.

Add chicken wings to bag a few at a time and shake to coat them with flour mixture. Place coated wings on baking sheet and refrigerate for an hour.

Melt butter and stir in hot sauce. Dip wings into butter-hot sauce mixture and return to baking sheet. Bake chicken until no longer pink, about 30-45 minutes depending on the size of the wings. Turn wings after they have baked about 15-20 minutes to make sure they are done evenly on all sides.

Buffalo Chicken Dip

Cost $15
Prep Time 30 minutes

I first had this at a jewelry party at a friend's home. I kept chipping and dipping on this until I bought some bling bling. I came out with a few pairs of earrings and a great recipe!

1 8-ounce block cream cheese, softened
½ cup hot wing sauce
½ cup blue cheese or ranch dressing
2 cups chopped or shredded cooked chicken
½ cup blue cheese or shredded cheddar cheese, depending on how much you like the flavor of blue cheese

Preheat oven to 350. Combine all ingredients in a 2-quart casserole dish or oven-safe serving dish. Bake 20 minutes or until heated through.

If you'd rather heat this in a Crock Pot, which would keep it toasty during your party, mix ingredients in Crock Pot and heat on low for about 30 minutes to an hour or until heated through.

Serve with your favorite dippers. Tortilla chips, Fritos Scoops and celery sticks and baby carrots are great go-alongs.

Annie Oeth   Photo credit: © 2014 Melanie Thortis

3

If you are what you eat, then I am cheap, fast and easy: Quick Dinners To Save Your Sanity

Getting It On

I'm not being naughty or referring to Marvin Gaye's famous song. I am talking about the daily challenge of getting dinner on.

Alas, getting it on is neither fun nor easy most nights. If the "It" of "Let's Get It On" is dinner, then getting it on takes a little thought and effort.

First, you have to have an idea, and those are hard to come by. Otherwise you will be wandering the supermarket aisles aimlessly, hoping something delicious and nutritious that your family will love will jump into your cart. That rarely happens.

Weeknight dinners are a challenge today.

Used to be, our mamas would have dinner on the table about 6 p.m., just as the local TV news would come on. There'd be chicken-fried steak, a pot roast, spaghetti or a casserole, plus a couple of vegetables, rolls or cornbread, plus dessert.

I will tell you that we grew up in a simpler time. Our mamas were stay-at-home moms, for the most part, and we kids didn't have nearly the activities today's children do. Sports leagues, dance classes, martial arts and the like keep families on the go.

As my friend Terre said once, "When you open the door to your minivan, and fast-food wrappers fall out, you know your family is doing too much."

The fast food is too easy some nights.

For starters, there is the laziness factor, because I do hit a point in the evening when I want anything for dinner that doesn't involve me cooking it.

Then there is the fact that your children will rise up and call you blessed when you bring home takeout or fast food. Your name could be Rachel Ray, Betty Crocker or Guy Fieri, but I guarantee your children would still shout hooray over takeout.

The kids just seem to run to the door, happily singing my praises, if I come in at the end of the day with a pizza in my hands.

Mine have even used psychology on me to get me to call in the order.

"Mom, you work so hard," one of the kids would say. "You deserve a break. Wouldn't you like to put your feet up and relax?"

Heck, yeah, I'd like to put my feet up, so that argument always works on me. Always.

But we can't eat takeout all the time. If we did, I'd just end up with less cash and more butt. Not a pretty picture.

With that in mind, I'm offering up some ideas to help get you through the crunch time and into the dinner hour.

Meals Your Family Will Eat

Step one: Take a pile of money. Step two: Set fire to it. Recipe for stupidity?

Well, cooking things your family will not eat is doing just about the same thing. A pile of money disappears, but by cooking things your family won't eat, you're also having to shop for groceries, bring them home, put them away, take them out again, cook them, clean up the kitchen, store the leftovers and then throw them away when they're old. I'm thinking this is pretty stupid.

But have I done this? Of course.

I see something that looks fantastic in a foodie magazine and don't stop to think about the likes or dislikes of my family. I'm in "Let's make dinner look like the picture in the book" mode.

There are alternative meals that will not make you crazy. Because what is the point of gathering your loved ones together for a meal cooked with love only to snap at them because you're exhausted. (Unfortunately, I have done this, too.)

These meals are also easy on the budget.

So here are some meals that most families, including kids, will eat. The recipes for the items with asterisks are included in this book.

Pork Chops and Rice*: This is quick, easy and good with a green vegetable, whether it comes from a can, the freezer or the produce section.

Tacos: Make it a feast by making Spanish rice (mix) and black beans (canned) to go with it.

Mexican pizzas: Take small flour tortillas (we like the low-carb ones), spread them with low-fat refried beans, drizzle with salsa and top with seasoned ground beef for tacos (follow seasoning envelope directions) and shredded cheese. Bake at 350 for about 7-10 minutes or until cheese is melted. Serve with shredded lettuce, chopped tomatoes, sour cream, guacamole or your family's favorite taco toppings.

Spaghetti*, Pizza Casserole*, Lasagna or Three Cheese Casserole*: The combination of Italian-inspired pasta plus salad is a crowd-pleaser that's nice enough for company. Serve with your favorite tossed green salad and garlic bread.

Chili*: Make a Crock Pot of this and pair it up with cornbread or corn muffins. Serve brownies topped with a scoop of vanilla ice cream and a drizzle of chocolate syrup for dessert.

Poppyseed Chicken*: This pale-colored dish is delicious with colorful sides such as fruit salad (Cut up cantaloupe, strawberries, fresh or canned pineapple, or purchase fruit salad in your supermarket's produce section), cooked and buttered carrots, baked sweet potatoes , green beans and the like. This can be prepared ahead of time, so all you would have to do is pop it in the oven when you're making the rest of dinner.

Breakfast for dinner I: pancakes or waffles (use your favorite mix), bacon or sausage, orange juice and/or milk

Breakfast for dinner II: Scrambled eggs or Cheese Omelets*, bacon or sausage, toast or Biscuits* with orange juice and/or milk

Fried chicken*: Serve with your family's favorite fixings. We like Macaroni and Cheese* and green beans, or pasta salad or potato salad (make your favorite or stop by your supermarket's deli counter) plus a green salad (toss your favorite kind or pick up one of those handy salad kits in the produce section.)

Meatloaf*: Now we're talking comfort food. Serve this with homemade mashed potatoes (totally worth the effort) and peas (LeSueur is our favorite).

Baked ham: Pair this up with a potato casserole, using either white or sweet potatoes, and English peas or green beans plus rolls (Try Sour Cream Rolls*). A plus is that you'll have leftovers.

Pot Roast*: Check out the recipes in the Crock Pot section. I have a child who loves gravy, so I try to always have au jus or gravy to serve, either on top of potatoes and carrots cooked with the roast or with mashed potatoes.

Sloppy Joes: Brown and drain one pound of lean ground beef seasoned with dried minced onions. Return meat to skillet and simmer with about ½ cup ketchup. Serve on hamburger buns. Popular sides to this at our house are baked French fries or Tater Tots (pick up your favorite kind from the supermarket's freezer section) and mini cobs of corn (get these in the freezer section, too).

Hamburgers: If the weather's nice, cook these on your grill, or broil or panfry hamburger patties in the house. Add cheese if you want. Serve these on toasted buns with your favorite toppings and condiments. Serve with French Fries or Baked Beans*.

German Sausage and Potatoes*: This can be ready in 30 minutes, easy. Serve up with something colorful, such as corn on the cob or a green salad. You can prepare these while the potatoes cook.

Barbecued Chicken: If you are pinched for time near the dinner hour, here's a hack: Boil bone-in chicken pieces until done but not falling off the bone. Then grill them, brushing with your favorite bottled barbecue sauce in the last 10 minutes. Pieces that work best for this method are breasts and leg quarters. No more worrying that your chicken will be under cooked. Serve with Baked Beans* and Potato Salad*, either using the recipe in this book or picking up something from the supermarket deli counter.

Brats: A Midwestern delicacy that can be cooked ahead to make your life easier. Simmer one package of brats in a skillet filled with one 12-ounce bottle of beer until sausages are done. From there, refrigerate until you are ready to grill. Grill sausages to brown the outsides and warm them. You can also grill hotdogs at the same time, if you have some children who aren't bratwurst fans. Serve on buns with Baked Beans* or baby carrots with Ranch dressing.

Leftovers

I love leftovers. I mean, who wouldn't?

Oh, wait, I know those who wouldn't. My children.

Why is it that those who don't cook or pay for groceries are the very ones who don't like leftovers? And y'all know I am telling the truth.

Leftovers are a favorite of mine because I get a night off from cooking. And not only do I not have to cook, but the kitchen stays cleaner and there are fewer dishes to wash.

Some meals are better the second time around. This is true of spaghetti, chili, taco soup, vegetable beef soup, Beef Lombardi and Baked Ziti. Foodies would say that the flavors "marry." I say, if those flavors don't marry, they at least go steady. The tastes of those dishes improve with time.

Leftovers might as well be money. Making good use of them gets the most out of your food dollar, plus it will save you money if, for example, you have leftovers for lunch instead of heading to the fast food drive-through.

There are ways to get your crew interested in leftovers. Here are a few ideas.

- Bake bread. A quick bread, such as Beer Muffins, Mayonnaise Rolls, Sour Cream Rolls, biscuits or cornbread, will do. Hot, fresh bread makes the rest of the meal more appealing.

- Change up the sides. Add a fresh salad, some baby carrots and Ranch dip or fresh fruit.

- Make dessert special. Even something as simple as a lemon ice box pie or a pan of brownies from a mix (Ghirardelli mixes are particularly indulgent) will make a meal more of a celebration.

- Cook ahead. That's right, plan those leftovers. For example, bake a chicken for dinner, but bake an extra one and use the meat a couple of nights later for chicken salad or chicken quesadillas.

- Load potatoes. Making a glazed ham? Chop up some of the ham leftovers and save them for this. Bake potatoes, scoop out the pulp and mash like you're making Whooped Taters, only add in ham, cheese, and green onion. Spoon potatoes back into the potato shells, topping with shredded cheese and bake at 350 until cheese is melted.

Hamburger Steaks
with Rice and Gravy
Serves 4
Cost $8
Prep Time 30 minutes

1 pound ground beef
1 can Cream of Mushroom soup
Salt and pepper
Rice

This recipe is one I learned in college, and it is pure comfort food that's quick, easy and also not so rough on the pocketbook. My children have loved this recipe so much that my middle son called home from his college apartment to ask me how to make this.

Start preparing rice according to package directions. While the rice is cooking, prepare the hamburger steaks.

Form ground beef info four patties and brown in a skillet, seasoning with salt and pepper and turning occasionally until done. Remove hamburger steaks from skillet and drain fat from skillet. Wipe with a paper towel to remove more fat. Add can of Cream of Mushroom soup to skillet, adding water as necessary to make gravy to desired consistency. Stir to smooth out any lumps.

Add hamburger steaks back to skillet and let simmer in gravy until rice is done.

To serve, place rice on center of plate and top with a hamburger steak and plenty of mushroom gravy.

Chicken and White Bean Chili
Serves 4-6
Cost $8
Prep Time 20 minutes / Cook Time 20 minutes

This is one of the Dear Daughter's favorite meals, and it's so quick and easy that it's a weekday/school day/work day favorite. It's also delicious and warming on a cold day.

   1 pound boneless skinless chicken, sliced into
      bite-size pieces
   1 onion, chopped
   1 can chopped green chilies
   1 can Great Northern Beans, drained
   1 envelope white gravy mix (or country gravy mix)
   2-3 bouillon cubes

In soup pot or Dutch oven, sauté onion and chicken over medium heat until chicken is no longer pink and onion is softened.

Stir in undrained can of chopped green chilies and beans. Prepare three cups bouillon and add to pot with chicken, onions and chilies.

In small mixing bowl, whisk gravy mix with 1 cup water until smooth. Stir this into the pot to thicken soup. Add more water if necessary. Simmer about 15-20 minutes on low. This is delicious garnished with a dollop of sour cream, a sprinkle of grated Mexican cheese blend or both!

Chicken Dinner in a Flash

Cost $10

Prep Time 30 minutes

1 pound boneless, skinless chicken breasts
Teriyaki sauce
1 package chicken-flavored rice mix
1 can green beans, cut or French cut
1 can pear halves
Mayonnaise, light or regular
Shredded cheese

Place your chicken breasts in a shallow dish. Prick them with a fork. Sprinkle with teriyaki sauce and marinate for about 10 minutes.

While chicken marinates, put rice on to cook according to package directions. I like to use the microwave version on the package, as this is one less thing to babysit on the stovetop.

While rice cooks and chicken marinates, drain pear halves and place them on a plate. Top each half with a spoonful of mayonnaise. Sprinkle liberally with shredded cheese. Refrigerate until ready to serve.

Open can of green beans. Warm in saucepan on stovetop on the low setting, seasoning with salt, pepper and butter as desired.

Take chicken and grill, broil or bake. This should take about 30 minutes, depending on the thickness of the chicken. Serve chicken with rice, green beans and pear salads.

Taco Pie
Cost $12
Prep Time 45 minutes

This recipe is a great reason to keep a box of Bisquick around. It's easy, delicious and a hit with the kids.

1 pound ground beef
1 onion, chopped
1 envelope taco seasoning
1 can chopped green chilies
2 eggs
1 cup milk
½ cup Bisquick
¾ cup shredded cheese, cheddar or Mexican
  four-cheese blend
Thinly sliced lettuce
Chopped tomatoes
Salsa
Sour cream

Preheat oven to 400. Spray a pie pan with nonstick cooking spray. In skillet, brown ground beef and onions until done and drain. Return to skillet and season with taco seasoning. Spoon beef mixture into pie plate. Top beef mixture with chilies.

In mixing bowl, beat eggs and add milk and Bisquick, stirring until blended. Pour on top of beef and chilies.

Bake for about 25 minutes. Top with cheese and bake for about five more minutes or until cheese is melted. Slice and serve with tomatoes, lettuce, sour cream and salsa.

Shepherd's Pie

Cost $12

Prep Time 25 minutes / Bake Time 20 minutes

About a pound of potatoes
1 onion, chopped
1 green pepper, chopped
1 pound ground beef
Salt and pepper
Shredded cheddar cheese
Milk
Butter or margarine

Preheat oven to 350 degrees.

Peel potatoes and cut them into chunks. In large saucepan or pot, boil potatoes until tender.

While potatoes boil, brown ground beef with chopped onion and green pepper. Drain and season meat with salt and pepper.

Spray your favorite casserole dish with nonstick cooking spray. Put meat in casserole dish.

Drain boiled potatoes and whip with electric mixer, adding milk and butter to make Whooped Taters. Season with salt and pepper to taste.

Top meat with potatoes, and sprinkle cheese on top of potatoes. Bake at 350 for about 20 minutes or until top of casserole is lightly browned.

Meatloaf Dinner in a Flash

Cost $15

Prep Time 15 minutes / Bake Time 30 minutes

1 pound ground beef
1 envelope onion soup mix
¼ cup oatmeal, uncooked
1 egg
¼ cup milk
Barbecue sauce (your favorite)
1 box macaroni and cheese mix (your favorite)
1 bag frozen peas
1 box brownie mix (your favorite)

The trick to this is to make your meatloaves small, either by hand or in a muffin pan. Smaller meatloaves cook faster.

Preheat oven to 400. In mixing bowl, mix ground beef, onion soup mix, oatmeal, egg and milk until well blended. Either form small loaves and place on broiler pan or place meat in a muffin pan that has been sprayed with nonstick cooking spray. Bake for about 30 minutes or until done.

Meanwhile, prepare macaroni according to package directions. Shells and cheese is a favorite at our house, but go with what your crew enjoys most.

While pasta boils, put on frozen peas, either in a microwave dish, steam in the bag if you bought that kind, or simmer in water in a saucepan according to package directions.

61

While peas and pasta cook, stir together brownie mix and pour into an 8-inch-by-8-inch square pan that has been sprayed with nonstick cooking spray. Set aside.

Finish cooking macaroni and place in a serving bowl. Pour cooked peas into a serving bowl.

Take mini meatloaves out of oven to drain away grease. Glaze with barbecue sauce and place them on a serving plate.

Adjust oven temperature to accommodate your brownies, going by what the box says. Let brownies bake while you serve dinner.

When your family is done eating the entrée, there will be warm brownies for dessert. As they used to say on those old "A-Team" episodes on television, I just love it when a plan comes together.

Istockphoto.com\sartorisliterary /© bhofack2

Catfish in a Hurry

Cost $12

Prep Time 15 minutes / Bake 20-30 minutes

1 package of catfish fillets, enough for your family
Bottled ranch salad dressing
Parmesan cheese, grated
Frozen corn on the cob
Zucchini, yellow summer squash or a mix of both
Olive oil
Salt and pepper

Preheat oven to 400. Place fish fillets in a 9-inch-by-13-inch pan that has been sprayed with nonstick cooking spray. Drizzle fish fillets with ranch dressing. Sprinkle with parmesan cheese.

Take squash and cut into halves or fourths, depending on the size of the squash. Drizzle with olive oil and season with salt and pepper to taste. Place on baking sheet.

Put corn on the cob in large saucepan and boil on stove or microwave in a covered microwave-safe dish until done, following package directions.

Bake fish and squash for about 20-30 minutes, or until squash is crisp-tender and fish flakes easily.

Place fish and veggies in serving dishes, and you're ready for dinner. If you're serving this during the summer, which is a great idea since squash will be in season, you can offer ice cream or ice cream sandwiches for dessert.

German Sausage and Potatoes
Cost $10
Prep Time 45 minutes (including cooking)

1 pound smoked sausage or kielbasa, sliced
2-3 sliced green onions
About 5 medium to large potatoes, depending
  on the size of your family
¼ cup Italian salad dressing
½ cup shredded cheddar cheese

Preheat oven to 350. Peel and cut potatoes into bite-size chunks. Boil potatoes until done and drain. In large mixing bowl, combine boiled potatoes, sliced smoked sausage, sliced green onions, Italian dressing and grated cheddar cheese. Put mixture into 9-inch-by-13-inch baking dish and bake for about 15-20 minutes or until heated through and cheese is melted.

Three-Cheese Casserole
Cost $15
Prep Time 30 minutes / Bake 30 minutes

1 pound ground beef
Garlic powder, salt and pepper to taste
1 tsp. sugar
2 8-ounce cans tomato sauce
4 green onions, chopped
1 cup sour cream
8 ounces cream cheese, softened
8 ounces cottage cheese
8 ounces egg noodles, cooked and drained
½ cup shredded cheddar cheese or shredded
  cheese blend

This is also called Husband's Delight Casserole, not to be confused with the dessert of the same name.

Whatever you call it, it's fantastic.

Brown ground beef and drain. Return meat to skillet and simmer with seasonings and tomato sauce. Meanwhile, in mixing bowl, blend sour cream, cream cheese, cottage cheese, onions and noodles. Spray a casserole dish with nonstick cooking spray, and place noodles in casserole. Top with meat sauce. Top meat sauce with cheese. Bake at 350 for 20-30 minutes or until cheese is melted and casserole is heated through.

Lauren's Chicken Fried Rice
Cost $8
Prep and Cook Time 45 minutes

1 cup long-grain rice
1 egg
½ onion, chopped
½ small bag frozen peas and carrots
1 pound boneless skinless chicken, cut into
  bite-size strips
Soy sauce

Tip on this recipe: You can make this even quicker
and easier by planning ahead. If you have chicken and rice
earlier in the week, cook extra of both and you are several
steps ahead toward having this recipe done.

Cook 1 cup long-grain rice in 2 cups water according
to package directions.

Meanwhile, spray a skillet with nonstick cooking
spray. Saute chicken until done and set aside.

In skillet, scramble one egg and set cooked egg aside.

In same skillet, spraying again with nonstick cooking
spray if necessary, sauté onion until translucent. Add peas
and carrots and continue to sauté for about 5-10 minutes or
until done.

Fold in cooked rice, cooked chicken and cooked egg,
blending to mix. Season with desired amount of soy sauce,
either regular or reduced sodium.

Sausage, Peppers and Penne

Cost $12

Prep and Cook Time 30 minutes

Penne pasta
1 package Italian sausage, hot or mild, about five links
1 onion, cut into strips
2-3 peppers, green, yellow, red or orange, cut into strips
1 small jar Marinara sauce

Cook desired amount of penne pasta according to package directions and drain.

In a skillet, simmer sausages in water until done and drain. Return sausages to skillet and brown. Remove and set aside.

Saute onions and peppers until tender. Return sausage to skillet. Cut sausage up into bite-sized pieces if desired.

Add marinara sauce. Serve meat, onions, peppers and sauce with penne pasta for a meal.

Tostadas

Usually, when your child declares, "Guess what!" you won't think what follows is nearly as cool as he does. At least, at first.

What followed the "Guess what!" one evening at our house was the third Dear Son saying, "I told my Spanish class you'd make tostadas for us."

"Sure," I said. Never mind that I had never eaten a tostada before, let alone made one.

I knew it was a Mexican dish, and figured that beans, cheese and maybe beef were involved, and probably tortillas. Since those are the building blocks of quite a few Mexican dishes, it was a safe guess.

The problem with never having eaten a tostada is that might mean I wouldn't know a good one from a bad one, so I left this to my taste buds.

Then I found out that there were twenty-something people in his Spanish class.

I am a woman of my word, though, and if I say I am going to make something I've never made before or eaten before for a classroom full of high-scholars, then I'll do it.

We looked up recipes, tweaked them until we had a plan we liked and then made a batch for dinner as a trial run. Then we kept on making them so we had some to bring to the high school Spanish class.

A tostada is like a layered Mexican pizza, so we fried up tortillas and packed them in gallon-sized zippered plastic bags. Then we had disposable containers of refried beans, salsa, shredded Mexican four-cheese blend, sour cream, thinly sliced lettuce, chopped tomatoes and guacamole all packed up to go. Yes, I love my boy a lot.

Everyone loved our tostadas, and you can add in ground beef, seasoned as for tacos, to the layers. Turns out, they are easy to make, too, and fun for a week night. If you have picky people in your family, this is perfect, as each person can make his own tostada.

Titan Tostadas

Cost $20
Prep and Cook Time 45 minutes

8 flour tortillas, small enough to fit in whatever
  skillet you plan to use
1 pound ground beef
1 envelope taco seasoning
1 can refried beans
Salsa (your favorite store-bought kind)
Mexican four-cheese blend shredded cheese
1 container guacamole (I am not a huge fan of
  store-bought guacamole, but we are going for ease)
Sour cream
Thinly sliced lettuce
Tomatoes, chopped

Spray a skillet with nonstick cooking spray and heat
over medium heat on the stovetop. Fry each tortilla on
each side until crispy, a few minutes on each side. Remove
crispy tortilla and set aside.

Brown ground beef and drain. Prepare with taco
seasoning, following package directions.

Open can of refried beans and warm in saucepan on
stovetop, using a medium to low setting.

Set out lettuce, tomatoes, sour cream, guacamole,
salsa and cheese in serving bowls, and do same with
seasoned beef and refried beans.

To serve, give each person a crispy tortilla. From
there, they can go to town, adding whatever they like.

4

The Crock Pot:
Your Secret Weapon

Your Very Own Secret Weapon

Sometime during the 1970s, back when women started bringing home the bacon, frying it up in a pan and singing about it on TV commercials, came the advent of Crock Pots, slow cookers and the like.

The idea of the Crock Pot was that you load the thing with chuck roasts, chickens and such, leave for a day of being a Fortune 500 executive, and when you get home, the pot roast and potatoes are done. It is a brilliant idea.

I got a mini Crock Pot as a wedding gift, starting my love affair with slow cooking.

The mini, which was great for two chicken breasts or a batch of Rotel dip, didn't prove large enough. So then I got the full size Crock Pot in a brownish shade.

A few years down the road, I was given a slow cooker that wanted to scorch things, so I went back to the tried and true Crock Pot. There is a difference between the two. A slow cooker is a pan that sits on top of a flat heating element. The Crock Pot, on the other hand, a product of Rival, is a piece of pottery that sits inside a bowl-shaped heating element.

Some people have had great results with slow cookers, but not me. After a few batches of Rote dip that were scorched on the bottom, I was ready to go back to Crock Potting.

The brown Crock Pot gave up the ghost, so then came a $20 green one with ivy decorations on the heating element. It got used to the point of ugliness, so I bought a

72

white one that got used to the point of the pot springing a leak. I then bought a $20 replacement, a black one with a jacquard pattern.

These Crock Pots reflect the styles of the day, from rustic browns of the mid 1980s to hunter green circa 1990 to a styling black from 2014. It's nice that, while gas is approaching $4 a gallon at times, the price of Crock Pots, the basic ones that have the settings of off, low, high and warm, are still about $20.

What's so great about them?

You can set them and leave the house, knowing that, unless you forgot to plug it in, the Crock Pot will cook your dinner while you are out working.

You can cook large quantities of recipes, again, without babysitting a pot.

Tougher cuts of meat turn out tender.

They're versatile.

You can take them tailgating as long as you have somewhere to plug them in.

They're an inexpensive wedding gift.

College students love them for their off-campus apartments. My middle dear son got one in his grad school days and found that he could feed a lot of people without a lot of effort with his handy, dandy Crock Pot.

And finally, nothing is more comforting than to walk in the door at the end of the day to the aroma of dinner that's ready and waiting for you.

Here are a few ideas to get you Crock Potting happily.

Creamy Italian Chicken

Serves 4-6
Cost $12
Prep Time 5 minutes / Simmer 6-8 hours

1 pound boneless, skinless chicken breasts
1 8-ounce package of cream cheese
(regular or reduced fat)
1 envelope Italian salad dressing mix
1 package sliced fresh mushrooms
Pasta (I like penne or bowties, but use your favorite)

Place chicken in the bottom of the Crock Pot. Top with cream cheese, dressing mix and mushrooms. Cover and cook on low about 6-8 hours. When you get home from the office, errands or the mall, stir the chicken and boil the pasta.

This is excellent with a green salad and garlic bread. Serve with your favorite white wine, and it is company worthy.

Can-Can Spaghetti Sauce
Serves 6-8
Cost $10
Prep Time 15 minutes / Simmer 30-40 minutes

1 pound ground beef, browned and drained
2 cans Italian seasoned diced tomatoes
2 cans tomato paste
1 can mushrooms
1-2 tsp. Italian seasoning blend
1-2 tsp. sugar
Red wine (optional)

Blend ingredients in the Crock Pot, adding a few tablespoons of red wine if desired. Cook on low for about 8 hours and serve on your favorite pasta. Add salad and garlic bread to make this a meal. And the rest of the red wine, if you have grown-ups coming to dinner. Note: You can also do this one on the stovetop, simmering for about 30-40 minutes on low instead of going the Crock Pot route.

Mushroom and Onion Pot Roast

Serves 4-6

Cost $15

Prep Time 10 minutes / Simmer 8 hours

1 chuck roast
Salt and pepper
1 can cream of mushroom soup
1 envelope onion soup mix
3-4 potatoes (I like red-skinned ones or new potatoes),
  washed and quartered
Baby carrots, about a handful or more if you like

Place roast in Crock Pot, and season with salt and pepper if desired. In small bowl, mix soup and soup mix and spread over roast. Add potatoes and carrots. Cover and cook for 8 hours. Note: Less-expensive cuts, such as English roasts or chuck roasts, are great for this recipe.

Mustard and Onion Pot Roast
Serves 4-6
Cost $10
Prep Time 5 minutes / Cook 6-8 hours

1 chuck roast
Mustard
Dried minced onions or fresh onions, chopped

This recipe is a little less expensive than the Mushroom and Onion Pot Roast, and believe it or not, it does not have a mustard flavor. Instead, it comes out with a delicious au jus that you can serve atop mashed potatoes. Or serve the meat on toasted rolls and use the au jus as a dipping sauce to make homemade French Dip Sandwiches.

Place roast in Crock Pot. Spread meat with mustard and top with onions. Cover and cook on low 6-8 hours.

A note on using dried minced onions: As a mom of young children, I discovered dried minced onions. It was like the discovery of fire. OK, it wasn't that big a deal, but dried minced onions are inexpensive, small (key for sneaking them past onion-hating children), last in your cabinet for a while (no tossing out produce that's gone bad) and are easy. Just shake them into your recipe. I realize that the "Top Chef" judges would not OK this, but how many of them cook dinner with a baby on the hip or teenagers to shuttle here and there?

Chili for Michael
Serves 8-10
Cost $10
Prep Time 15 minutes / Cook 6 hours

My youngest son, Michael, has never been a big fan of chunks of tomato in chili, while I happen to love them. But I love him more, so I will whip up a batch of chili for him that's smoother. You're welcome, sweetie.

- 1 pound ground beef, browned and drained
- 3 cans chili beans, hot or mild
- 4 cups tomato juice
- ½ tsp. garlic powder
- ½ tsp. salt
- ¼ tsp. pepper
- ½-1 tsp. chili powder, or to taste
- ¼ tsp. hot sauce

Combine all ingredients in Crock Pot. Cover and cook on low about 6 hours. This is good on top of corn chips and topped with cheese (your own homemade Frito chili pie!), and we also like topping this with a dollop of sour cream and maybe a few pickled jalapeno slices.

Baked Potatoes
Serves 4-6
Cost $4
Cook 4-8 hours

Potatoes, either russets or sweet potatoes

Allow one potato per person. Wash potatoes and place them in Crock Pot. They should not be pierced. You can wrap them in aluminum foil if desired, but I have had good results without the foil.

Cover and cook on low for about 4-8 hours, depending on the size of the potatoes.

Once I learned that I could bake potatoes in the Crock Pot, I never went back to baking them in the oven. You'll keep your kitchen cooler, and I have never had a potato come out with any underdone hard spots.

In the summer, we've had these Crock Pot Baked Potatoes for lunch with toppings such as chili or broccoli and cheese. Have potatoes cooked all day, and if you plan to grill on a summer evening, the potatoes are ready when you are.

At Thanksgiving and Christmas, when you're more likely to be making sweet potato pies and casseroles, this is an easy, no-fuss way to cook sweet potatoes to add to your recipes.

Taco Soup

Serves 6-8

Cost $15

Prep Time 15 minutes / Cook 6-8 hours

1 pound ground beef, browned and drained
1 envelope taco seasoning
1 envelope ranch dressing mix
1 can Rotel tomatoes and chilies
1 can diced tomatoes
1 can kidney beans, drained
1 can whole-kernel corn, golden or shoe peg, drained
1 can black beans, drained
1 12-ounce cans beer

Combine browned beef and other ingredients in your Crock Pot and stir. Cover and cook on low for 6-8 hours.

This is delicious topped with a dollop of sour cream and shredded cheddar-jack cheese and served with corn chips or tortillas or with cornbread.

Saucy Hamburger Steak

Serves 4-6

Cost $10-$12

Prep Time 5 minutes / Cook 6-8 hours

1 package tenderized cube steak, allowing 1-2 steaks
  per person
Salt
Pepper
1 can golden mushroom soup or cream of mushroom
  soup
Baby carrots (optional)
Small red-skinned potatoes, quartered (optional)

I grew up eating these budget cuts of meat, and they can be a little on the tough side, even with the tenderizing. My friend Kathy Matheny shared this recipe with me, and these come out tender and delicious and don't involve the babysitting of pan-frying or the extra calories and fat.

Season steaks and place in Crock Pot. Top with your choice of canned soup.

If desired, add potatoes and carrots for an easy one-pot meal. Or serve with rice or mashed potatoes so you can enjoy the flavorful mushroom gravy.

"Roasted" Hotdogs
Serves 4-8
Cost $5
Cook 45 minutes to 1 hour

Hotdogs
Buns

I realize that hotdogs can be microwaved in a minute or less or boiled in 10, but the Crock Pot can give you hotdogs with a roasted flavor. Simply place them in the Crock Pot and cover. No liquids are needed. Cook on high for about 45 minutes to an hour. The hotdog buns can be steamed by placing them on top of the hotdogs inside the Crock Pot for a few minutes just before serving.

Crock Pot Fajitas
Serves 6-8
Cost $10-$12
Prep Time 10 minutes / Cook 6-8 hours

**1-2 pounds boneless skinless chicken breasts
 or round steak
1 envelope fajita seasoning
1 onion, sliced
1 green pepper, sliced
¼ cup water
Tortillas**

Slice chicken or steak into strips and add all
ingredients to Crock Pot. Cover and cook on low for 6-8
hours. Serve with tortillas, salsa, sour cream, cheese and
other favorite fajita toppings. This is great with Mexican
rice and beans as sides.

Rotel Dip Three Ways
Serves 8-10 for snacking
Cost Under $10
Prep Time 15 minutes / Cook 2-4 hours

Rotel Dip is the go-to dip. My Midwestern sister-in-law, after I gave her the recipe, said, "What's Rotel?" Bless her heart. Can you imagine not having Rotel, that spicy canned blend of tomatoes and chili peppers?

Recipe 1: The Basic
1 pound Velveeta
1 can Rotel

Cube the Velveeta and add it and Rotel to the Crock Pot. Cook on low for 2-4 hours, stirring occasionally, until cheese is melted. Serve with tortilla chips.

Recipe 2: Rotel Blanco
2 8-ounce packages cream cheese
1 pound bulk pork sausage, mild or hot
1 can Rotel

Brown sausage and drain. Add to Crock Pot with cream cheese and Rotel. Cover and cook on low for about 2-4 hours, stirring occasionally, until cheese is melted. Serve with Triscuits.

Recipe 3: Chili Cheese Dip

1 can chili without beans
1 pound Velveeta
1 can Rotel

Cube Velveeta and add to Crock Pot with Rotel and canned chili. Cover and cook on low for about 2-4 hours, stirring occasionally, until cheese is melted. Serve with corn chips or tortillas.

Drunk Weenies
Serves 8-10 for snacking
Cost $8
Prep Time 5 minutes / Cook 4 hours

1 pound cocktail smoked sausages
1 bottle barbecue sauce (your favorite brand)
1 small jar grape jelly
½ cup red wine

Combine in Crock Pot. Cover and cook on low for about 4 hours. This is always welcome at holiday gatherings, tailgates and Super Bowl parties. Serve with toothpicks. You can use this as a sobriety test: How many attempts does your party guest make in the game of stab the wienie with the toothpick?

Party Mix
Makes about three quarts
Cost $12
Prep Time 5 minutes / Cook 2-3 hours

3 cups thin pretzel sticks
4 cups Rice or Corn Chex or Crispix
4 cups Cheerios
1 can mixed nuts
¼ cup melted butter or margarine
1 tsp. garlic powder
1 tsp. celery salt
1 tsp. seasoned salt or Cajun seasoning
2 tsp. grated Parmesan cheese

Love Party Mix but hate bending to stir it in the oven to keep it from burning? Try making your Party Mix in the Crock Pot. Mix ingredients in a large bowl, tossing to coat pieces with butter and seasonings. Pour into Crock Pot. Cover and cook on low about two hours, stirring every half hour. Remove lid and continue cooking on low and stirring another 30-45 minutes.

Variation: Omit garlic powder, celery salt and seasoned salt. Add one envelope of Ranch dressing mix and about 2 cups of cheese-flavored snack crackers. Cook as directed. Store in covered container.

Homemade Applesauce
Serves 8-10
Cost $7
Prep Time 15 minutes / Cook 3-4 hours

If you want to make your home smell wonderful, this is the recipe for you. Enjoy this with pork chops, a pork roast or grilled chicken, or have this for dessert.

8 tart apples (Granny Smiths work well), peeled, cored and cut into chunks
1 tsp. cinnamon
½ cup water
½ to 1 cup sugar or cinnamon red hot candies, depending on preference of spice and sweetness

Combine ingredients in Crock Pot. Cover and cook for 8-10 hours on low or 3-4 hours on high.

Potato Soup
Serves 4-6
Cost $8 (plus toppings)
Prep Time 5 minutes / Cook 6-7 hours

This doesn't happen too often, but I made this recipe and got a hug from the Dear Daughter. She's thirteen, so that explains about the hugs. She loved this dinner, though. Make this and let your children give you hugs.

1 30-ounce bag frozen hash browns
½ cup chopped onion
¼ tsp. black pepper
2 cans chicken broth
1 can cream of chicken soup
1 block of cream cheese, softened

Toppings:
Real bacon bits
Sour cream
Shredded cheese
Chopped green onions

Combine all ingredients except cream cheese in Crock Pot. Cover and cook on low for about 6 hours. Stir in cream cheese and cook about 30 more minutes or until melted. Stir. Serve topped with a dollop of sour cream, green onions, bacon bits and shredded cheese, and you get all the yummy flavors of a loaded baked potato.

Baked Beans

Serve 6-8

Cost $10

Prep Time 15 minutes / Cook 4-6 hours

This is often a side at cookouts and barbecues, but it is meaty enough to stand alone.

1 pound ground beef
1 onion, chopped
1 green pepper, chopped
4 cans pork and beans, drained
¾ cup brown sugar
2 Tbsp. mustard
2 Tbsp. Worcestershire sauce
¾ cup ketchup
1 cup barbecue sauce

Brown ground beef with onion and pepper. Drain and add to Crock Pot. Add remaining ingredients except bacon and stir to combine. Cover and cook on low 4-6 hours.

Red Beans and Rice
Cost $10
Prep Time 5 minutes / Cook 8 hours

Serve this with garlic bread and a bag of your favorite tossed salad and you've got a quick and easy dinner.

2 cans kidney beans with liquid
1 can Rotel tomatoes and chilies
1 green pepper, chopped
1 envelope onion soup mix
1 pound smoked sausage, sliced

Add all ingredients to Crock Pot, and cook on low for about 8 hours or on high for about four hours. Serve over white rice.

5

Get Your Southern On: Cooking Down South

Fried Chicken 101

Mrs. Mary Ruth Hill made it her mission in life. If she was going to do anything in her Home Economics I class at Oak Hill Academy, she was going to teach her students to cut up and fry a chicken.

This made complete sense, because no self-respecting woman should be at a loss when it comes to dealing with a yard bird. If a girl knew how to fry a chicken, then she stood a better chance of finding a husband. He'd smell that bird frying, and his nose would lead him to true love.

If that didn't work? Well, the girl might be single, but she'd be eating well.

One of the best parts of Home Economics classes was that we could eat what we cooked. While the girls who stayed away from the kitchen were stuck eating in the school cafeteria, we'd be off in the Home Ec lab, eating our fried chicken and enjoying a few salads as sides.

More about salads in the South later, but let's just say that none of the salads we ate with our fried chicken involved lettuce. The only green thing in them was lime Jell-O.

Back to the birds, though. We girls had our hairnets and aprons on, and we were wielding knives. Kids in biology class dissected frogs, but we Home Ec girls were setting out to take apart some broiler/fryers.

Yes, there are cut-up chickens in the supermarket, but Mrs. Hill would have nothing to do with those. The chicken plants didn't do their cutting to suit her.

It was because they included part of the backbone in the thigh pieces, when anyone with a shred of Southerness would know that a chicken thigh ought to have just one bone.

We'd wince at the sound of the bones coming apart, but Mrs. Hill could make quick work out of cutting up a chicken. Two drumsticks, two thighs, two wings would drop into the plastic bowl, and then things would get interesting.

The chicken's ribs would get cut, starting the separation of the bird's back and front. Once the breast was separated, the pulley bone would be cut.

For the uninitiated, a pulley bone is the wishbone, and that upper part of the chicken breast would be cut off from the rest of the whole breast. This was another reason we were warned to keep away from those chickens cut up at the chicken plants. The plants do not include the pulley bone cut.

Then what was left of the breast was split into two parts. Mrs. Hill would fry the back, too, but nobody at my house likes the back. When I am in a frugal mood, the backs get saved in a freezer bag for soup-making later. When I don't feel frugal, they get tossed.

But you really didn't want to read about cutting up. You'd rather read about the frying.

There's a reason for that. Frying chicken well is an art form.

I found that out the first time I tried frying a chicken at home without being under the watchful eye of Mrs. Hill.

93

My chicken was absolutely beautiful. It was crispy and golden on the outside, like a picture from my Better Homes & Gardens Cookbook.

But it was pink and bloody inside.

If it was a steak, that would have been one thing, but back then, I was known for overcooking beef and undercooking chicken. Needless to say, neither is good.

The art comes from all the parts of this simple dish. Cutting the bird up just right comes first, and then you have to have the oil right. Medium to medium low and go slow. You can't rush good chicken unless you want it raw inside.

From there, you have your denominations, just like sects of a religion. There are those who believe in a buttermilk crust, and those who go lighter and crispier.

Some pop a lid on top of the frying chicken to have a softer crust, and others who'd sooner throw that lid out the window than have anything less than crunchy chicken.

Some put their seasonings into the flour, and others put the seasonings on the chicken before a dusting of flour.

Just like Baptists, Methodists and Presbyterians, these fried chicken sects get along fairly well. This is because we know the real heretics are those who make oven-fried chicken.

Oven-fried chicken is just baked chicken. Either fry the chicken or grill, bake, broil or boil it, but don't pretend you can fry chicken in the oven, because you can't.

So with all that said, here's how I fry chicken. I don't fry it for just anyone or on any old night because it's not exactly heart healthy. It also takes some babysitting. Watched pots may not boil, but an unwatched skillet of chicken grease will burst into a fireball.

This fried chicken is wonderful on picnics and as the main dish with potato salad and baked beans for summer suppers. It's also delicious cold the next day.

Fried Chicken

Cost $6
Prep and Cook Time 1 hour

One whole broiler/fryer
All-purpose flour
Salt
Pepper
Vegetable oil
Cut up and rinse chicken, drying pieces well

Heat oil on medium to medium-low heat in a skillet. Use your preference of nonstick, cast-iron or an electric skillet, but the plus of an electric skillet is that many times, all your chicken pieces can fit in to fry at once.

Season raw chicken with salt and plenty of black pepper. Then, having placed about ¾ cup to 1 cup of flour on a plate or shallow bowl, roll seasoned chicken in flour.

Cook chicken at about 350 degrees (a handy feature of using an electric skillet is setting the temperature), turning the pieces after about 5 to 7 minutes of frying. Use tongs as a fork will pierce the crust and let out the juices. Fry until done, which means about 20 minutes for a breast or about 10-12 minutes for a drumstick.

Methodists Love Poppy Seeds

Nobody does a chicken casserole the way United Methodists do. You'd think it would be part of the United Methodist Book of Discipline, but no.

Still, this recipe is pretty divine. I became a United Methodist as an adult, which was about the time I had what has become my go-to as far as chicken casseroles go: Poppy Seed Chicken.

This creamy, dreamy casserole shows up at just about every potluck and church supper. It freezes well for planning ahead and it is also trotted over to the homes of those who have had illnesses or deaths in the family. It is a complete and utter consolation.

This recipe is so good at showing the love of Christ that it would have been a reasonable stand-in for the loaves and fish. And it's easy enough to whip together that it could be considered a minor miracle.

Poppy Seed Chicken

Feeds about four, and never have I had leftovers
Cost $8
Prep Time 30-40 minutes / Bake 30 minutes

1 pound chicken breasts
1 can cream of chicken soup
1 cup sour cream
Poppy seeds
1 sleeve of Ritz crackers
½ cup butter or margarine, melted

Boil chicken until cooked throughout and debone, shredding chicken into bite-sized pieces. Set aside.

In a large mixing bowl, blend soup and sour cream, plus about 1-2 Tbsp. poppy seeds. Fold in chicken, and pour mixture into a casserole dish.

Crush Ritz crackers, and in a medium-sized mixing bowl, mix them with melted butter. Sprinkle the buttered crumbs over the casserole, adding a sprinkle of poppy seeds on top if desired. There might be enough poppy seeds in this to make you fail a drug test.

Bake at 350 degrees for about 30 minutes.

If freezing for future use, place in aluminum pan and wrap in heavy-duty foil after adding the crumb topping. Thaw in refrigerator before baking.

Rotel Chicken
Serves 4-6
Cost $10
Prep Time 30-40 minutes / Bake 30 minutes

This is a favorite of ours when served up with English peas or a tossed green salad and garlic bread. I like it because it's easy, feeds a crowd and keeps the number of ingredients to a minimum.

1 pound boneless skinless chicken breasts
1 can Rotel canned tomatoes and chilles
1 pound Velveeta
8 ounces Angel Hair pasta

In a large Dutch oven, boil chicken breasts until done, reserving the water. Remove chicken from water, and use water in pot to boil pasta according to package directions. Drain pasta and chop chicken into bite-sized pieces. Cube Velveeta and combine in a large bowl with undrained Rotel, chicken and pasta. Pour into a casserole dish that has been sprayed with nonstick cooking spray. Bake at 350 for about 30 minutes or until bubbly.

Chicken Pie

Cost $12

Prep Time 30-40 minutes / Bake 35-40 minutes

Cornbread topping:
1 cup yellow cornmeal
1/3 cup flour
1 ½ tsp. baking powder
1 Tbsp. sugar
½ tsp. salt
½ tsp. baking soda
2 Tbsp. oil
¾ cup buttermilk
1 egg
½ cup melted butter

Chicken filling:
2 Tbsp. butter
1 small onion, chopped
1 ¾ cup chicken broth
1 can cream of chicken soup
2 ½ cups cooked chicken, cut into bite-size pieces
 (You can plan ahead and cook extra chicken earlier
 in the week, or use leftovers)
Salt and pepper to taste
1 tsp. curry powder (optional)

Preheat oven to 375. Mix all cornbread ingredients together except for melted butter in a large mixing bowl. Stir until smooth.

Bake in a greased 8-inch square baking pan for about 20 minutes or until golden brown. Remove from oven and let cool.

Crumble cornbread and put three cups of crumbs in a mixing bowl. Pour melted butter in the mixing bowl and stir. Set aside.

In a medium-sized saucepan, heat butter on low and sauté onions until done. Add chicken broth, cream of chicken soup and seasonings. Stir until blended. Add chicken and stir.

Spray your favorite casserole dish with nonstick cooking spray. Pour in chicken filling, then top with buttered cornbread crumbs.

Bake at 350 for about 35-40 minutes.

Vegetable Beef Soup
Cost $8
Prep and Cooking Time 1-2 hours

1 container vegetable leftovers from freezer, or go into the canned foods area of your supermarket and pick out several different kinds of veggies, such as beans, peas and corn
1 pound ground beef
1 onion, chopped
2 cans diced tomatoes, or more, if you like a more tomato-y soup
2-3 medium-sized potatoes, peeled and diced
2-3 carrots, peeled and sliced
If you have celery and peppers on hand, chop those up

This is a thrifty soup. A friend of mine who has a big garden shared this with me. She'd prepare butter beans, green beans, corn and the like to go with her family's dinners, but instead of saving the leftovers in the refrigerator or tossing them, she placed them into a large plastic container and put them into the freezer. When the container became full, it was time to make soup.

In soup pot, brown ground beef and onion, and if you have them, celery and peppers. Drain and return meat to pot. Add vegetables, draining if you are using canned. Add canned tomatoes, undrained, potatoes and carrots, plus enough water to bring soup to desired consistency. Stir, and simmer until all vegetables are tender. Season to taste.

Beef Lombardi
Serves about 6-8
Cost $15
Prep Time 30 minutes / Bake 30 minutes

My middle son calls this casserole "Beef Vince Lombardi." I don't think the legendary football coach came up with this recipe, but you could always eat a plate of this while watching football. This is always a hit at our house, especially in the winter, and it goes well with green salad and garlic bread.

1 pound ground beef
1 14.5-ounce can diced tomatoes
1 can Rotel tomatoes with chilies
2 tsp. sugar
2 tsp. salt
¼ tsp. pepper
1 6-ounce can tomato paste
6 ounces, more or less, of egg noodles, boiled and drained
6 green onions, sliced
1 cup sour cream
1 cup cheddar cheese, shredded
1 cup mozzarella cheese, shredded

Preheat oven to 350. Brown ground beef and drain. Return beef to skillet and combine with next six ingredients. Simmer for about 15 minutes, stirring occasionally. Combine cooked noodles, sour cream and green onions. Put noodles in the bottom of a 9-inch-by-13-inch baking dish. Top with beef mixture, and then top beef with cheese. Bake for about 30 minutes or until bubbly.

Whooped Taters
Serves about 4

Cost $5
Cooking Time 30 Minutes

2 pounds potatoes, Idaho or Yukon Gold are fine
1 cup milk
Butter or margarine
Salt and pepper to taste, or kick it up a notch with
   your favorite Cajun seasoning

This is a mashed potato recipe, but my very Southern daddy called this dish "whooped taters." I am not going to pretend I never made instant mashed potatoes, but there is no comparison between instant potatoes and this buttery homemade recipe. This recipe is pure comfort when paired with meatloaf, pot roast or fried chicken, and you can serve it with the tiny LeSueur peas, making the potatoes into a bird's nest with the peas in the center.

Peel and boil potatoes until done. Drain. Place boiled potatoes in a mixing bowl, and get out your mixer. These are "whooped taters," not mashed. Beat potatoes, adding milk gradually, along with about 2 Tbsp. butter or margarine and desired seasoning. Stop beating when potatoes are fluffy, about 3-5 minutes. Top with another tablespoon of butter or margarine. My daughter likes this with more butter, mashing the potatoes until it forms a "melted butter swimming pool."

Pork Chops and Rice
Serves 4
Cost $10
Prep Time 30 minutes / Bake 20-30 minutes

This is an easy recipe we've been making for more years than I care to remember. Serve this up with rolls and green beans or broccoli, and you have dinner on the table.

> **4 boneless pork chops**
> **1 cup rice, uncooked**
> **1 can cream of chicken soup**
> **1 cup sour cream**

Preheat oven to 350. In a skillet sprayed with nonstick cooking spray, brown pork chops. While chops are browning, cook rice in two cups water or as directed on package.

Put browned chops aside.

In large mixing bowl, combine rice with sour cream and cream of chicken soup. Season with salt and pepper to taste.

Spray your favorite casserole dish with nonstick cooking spray. Spoon rice into casserole, and then top with pork chops.

Bake at 350 for 20-30 minutes or until chops are completely done and rice mixture is bubbly.

Mashed Potato Casserole
Serves about 6
Cost $5
Prep Time 30 minutes / Bake 30 minutes

This recipe is one of the few potato recipes you can get away with freezing ahead of time—a big plus during the holiday season!

1 recipe Whooped Taters
4 ounces cream cheese
1 tsp. onion powder
1 tsp. garlic powder
1 tsp. Cajun seasoning or seasoned salt
Paprika

Make your Whooped Taters, but beat in cream cheese along with milk and butter or margarine and seasonings. Spoon into your favorite casserole dish that has been sprayed with cooking spray. Dot with butter and sprinkle top with paprika.

Bake at 350 for about 30 minutes.

To freeze for serving later, skip the baking step and cover with aluminum foil. Freeze. To serve later, thaw in refrigerator and bake as directed.

Sweet Potato Casserole

Serves about 6-8

Cost $7

Prep Time 15 minutes after potatoes are cooked

Bake 30 minutes

Enough sweet potatoes to measure about 4 cups cooked
½ cup sugar
2 eggs, beaten
½ tsp. salt
4 Tbsp. butter
½ cup milk
½ tsp. vanilla

Topping
½ cup brown sugar
1/3 cup flour
3 Tbsp. butter
½ cup chopped pecans

This is a recipe you can start ahead of time. Put sweet potatoes in your Crock Pot and let them bake on low, covered, about 8 hours. Take potatoes out when done and let them cool. Slice open potatoes lengthwise, and scoop potato out of the peel. In large mixing bowl, mix sweet potatoes with remaining ingredients.

Spoon potatoes into a 9-inch-by-13-inch baking dish that has been sprayed with cooking spray.

Make streusel topping by combining brown sugar, flour, softened butter and pecans. Sprinkle this on top of potatoes, and bake at 325 for about 30 minutes or until topping is lightly browned.

Squash Casserole

Serves about 8
Cost $10
Prep Time 30 minutes / Bake 30 minutes

3 pounds squash, sliced
5 Tbsp. butter or margarine
1 onion, chopped
1 cup cheddar cheese, shredded
2 eggs, beaten
¼ cup mayonnaise
2 tsp. sugar
1 tsp. salt
About a sleeve of Ritz crackers, crushed

If you want to try your hand at gardening, grow squash. I have lived through bad years for squash, but most years, summer squash are prolific. One thing you can do with an abundance of squash is make this casserole. It's so good, I could make dinner off it.

Preheat oven to 350. Cook squash in a saucepan, boiling it for about 10 minutes. Then drain.

Saute' chopped onion in 4 Tbsp. butter or margarine until soft. Add drained squash and sauté about 5 minutes. In large mixing bowl, combine squash and onion mixture with remaining ingredients except for crushed Ritz crackers. Spoon into your favorite casserole dish, making sure to spray it with cooking spray.

Melt 1 Tbsp. butter and mix with cracker crumbs. Sprinkle on top of squash. Bake for about 30 minutes.

Green Beans, Southern Style
Serves about 6-8
Cost $8
Prep Time 15 minutes / Cook 6-9 hours

This is for when you grow green beans in your summer garden or hit the local farmer's market. So simple and so yummy.

About 2 pounds or eight cups of green beans, trimmed
About ¼ pound bacon, cut into pieces
1 onion, chopped

Salt and pepper to taste

Brown bacon in skillet and remove. Saute chopped onion in bacon grease. Add green beans to Crock Pot with seasonings, sautéed onion and bacon, which has been crumbled. Put in enough water to cover beans. Cover Crock Pot and cook beans on low for about 6-8 hours.

Green Bean Casserole
Serves about 6-8
Cost $5
Prep Time 5 minutes / Bake 30 minutes

My children would eat just about anything if you put a topping of Ritz crackers and butter on it. I would, too. This casserole is easy, delicious and can be made ahead of time and frozen.

3 cans French-cut green beans, drained
1 cup sour cream
1 can cream of mushroom soup
Salt and pepper to taste
About a sleeve of Ritz crackers, crushed
1 Tbsp. butter or margarine

Preheat oven to 350.

In large mixing bowl, combine green beans, sour cream, cream of mushroom soup, salt and pepper. Spoon into your favorite casserole dish that has been sprayed with cooking spray.

Melt butter or margarine and combine with crushed Ritz crackers. Sprinkle on top of green beans.

Bake for about 30 minutes.

If freezing ahead, prepare casserole, but instead of baking, cover with aluminum foil and freeze. Thaw in refrigerator when ready to use and bake as directed.

Hash Brown Casserole

Cost $10
Prep Time 10 minutes / Bake 40 minutes

1 2-pound package frozen hash brown potatoes
½ cup melted butter or margarine
1 can cream of chicken soup
1 8-ounce container sour cream
½ cup chopped onions
2 cups shredded cheddar cheese
Salt and pepper to taste
2 cups crushed corn flakes
½ cup melted butter or margarine

This casserole is a favorite at potluck suppers and goes so well with a glazed ham that I've put this on our Easter dinner table many times. Grilling? Serve this up as a side with steaks. The flavor is similar to twice-baked potatoes and is a great partner.

Preheat oven to 350. Spray your favorite 3-quart casserole dish with nonstick cooking spray. In large mixing bowl, combine hash brown potatoes, ½ cup melted butter or margarine, cream of chicken soup, sour cream, chopped onion, grated cheddar cheese, salt and pepper. Spoon mixture into casserole dish. Melt remaining butter or margarine and combine with cornflake crumbs in a mixing bowl. Sprinkle crumb mixture over top of casserole. Bake covered in a preheated oven for 40 minutes or until bubbly.

Chicken and Dressing

Serves about 8

Cost $12

Prep Time 15 minutes / Bake 1 hour

1 onion, chopped
1 cup chopped celery
¼ cup butter or margarine
1 ½ tsp. thyme
1 tsp. poultry seasoning
Salt and pepper to taste
2 eggs, beaten
1 package stuffing cubes
3 cups cubed rotisserie chicken or boiled chicken
1 can cream of chicken soup
1/3 cup water

Chicken and dressing was one of my favorites as a girl eating with my family at the Southern Inn in West Point, Mississippi. You'd get a scoop of dressing (scooped out with an ice cream scoop), topped with boiled chicken and gravy, with a little jellied cranberry sauce on the side.

Preheat oven to 350. In a large pot, sauté onion and celery in butter or margarine until soft. Remove from heat. Add broth, seasonings, eggs and bread cubes and stir. Spoon into a 9-inch-by-13-inch baking dish that has been sprayed with cooking spray. Top with chicken. Mix soup with water and pour over chicken. Cover with foil and bake for about 50 minutes. Uncover and bake another 5-10 minutes. Serve with canned jellied cranberry sauce and tiny LeSueur peas or green beans.

Corn Pudding
Serves about 6-8
Cost $3
Prep and Cook Time 40 minutes

I made this fairly regularly for holiday dinners, but one year I didn't. My oldest son acted like I had a fit of lunacy. How on earth could it be a holiday without Corn Pudding? Corn Pudding is his favorite casserole, and he could eat the whole bowl. I've made this so many times that the measurements are in my head.

2 cans cream corn
2 eggs, beaten
3 Tbsp. self-rising flour
1 ½ tsp. sugar
2 Tbsp. butter or margarine, melted
1 Tbsp. milk
Salt and pepper to taste

Preheat oven to 350. In large mixing bowl, combine cream corn, beaten eggs, seasonings, flour, butter and milk. Pour into your favorite casserole dish that has been sprayed with cooking spray. Bake 30 minutes or until casserole is set (not jiggly) and golden brown. Cool at room temperature for a few minutes before serving.

This dish is pretty with side dishes of contrasting colors, such as sliced fresh tomatoes, beets or green beans.

Macaroni and Cheese
Serves about 4
Cost $5
Prep and Cook Time 45 minutes

This is my own fault, but my children love the macaroni and cheese in the blue box better than the homemade kind. However, homemade macaroni and cheese is the ultimate comfort food to me.

I learned to make the homemade variety in high school home economics, but it has evolved a little since then. It pairs up well with fried chicken and meatloaf. It's substantial enough, though, to go it alone.

8 ounces elbow macaroni, or use your favorite pasta
2 Tbsp. butter or margarine
2 Tbsp. flour
Salt and pepper to taste
1 ½ cups milk
1 bag shredded Velveeta

Preheat oven to 350. Boil pasta according to package directions and drain.

In saucepan, melt butter or margarine. Whisk in flour, being careful to beat out any lumps. Whisk in milk and seasonings. With a wooden spoon, stir in cheese until melted. Stir in pasta, and pour mixture into your favorite casserole dish that has been sprayed with cooking spray. Bake for 30 minutes or until bubbly and golden brown.

Mexican Cornbread

Serves about 6

Cost $8

Prep Time 15 minutes / Bake 1 hour

1 cup butter, melted
1 cup white sugar
4 eggs
1 can cream corn
1 small can green chilies, drained
½ cup shredded Monterrey Jack cheese
½ cup shredded cheddar cheese
1 cup flour
1 cup yellow cornmeal
4 tsp. baking powder
¼ tsp. salt

My friend Raymond Reeves says, if you put sugar in cornbread, you might as well put frosting on it and call it a cupcake. But there are others, like my mama, who always put sugar in cornbread. I like cornbread any way you make it, but this recipe with sugar has a nice blend of sweetness and heat.

Preheat oven to 300. Spray a 9-inch-by-13-inch baking dish with nonstick cooking spray.

In large mixing bowl, beat together butter and sugar. Beat in eggs one at a time. Blend in cream corn, chilies and cheeses. Stir in flour, cornmeal, baking powder and salt. Pour batter into prepared dish.

Bake at 300 for 1 hour or until a toothpick inserted comes out clean or until bread bounces back to the touch.

Broccoli Bread
Serves about 8-10
Cost $6
Prep Time 15 minutes / Bake 40-45 minutes

I will tell you that only about two or three of us really enjoy broccoli, but that's OK with me. More broccoli bread for us! This is a sweet cornbread recipe, but it's delish. We like it with barbecued chicken, and it also goes well with soups and stews.

2 boxes Jiffy cornbread mix
2 Tbsp. margarine or butter
1 onion, chopped
4 eggs, beaten
4 cups fresh or frozen broccoli, chopped
  (thaw broccoli if using frozen)
1 cup cottage cheese
¼ cup milk

Preheat oven to 350. Spray a 9-inch-by-13-inch pan with nonstick cooking spray. Melt butter in skillet and sauté onion in butter until tender. In large mixing bowl, combine ingredients and mix well. Pour batter in pan and bake at 350 for about 40-45 minutes or until done.

6

Frozen Assets:
Cook ahead and take it easy

Feeding the Need

Every so often, some women's magazine will come up with a plan for cooking one day and eating dinner for a month. There have been recipe books written on the subject, and blog posts galore.

It's a brilliant idea, this cooking once and then not cooking the rest of the month.

The plusses are that you don't cook the rest of the month (duh), you don't have to grocery shopping for the month except for perishables such as fresh veggies and milk and you're prepared for anything.

When do I have to order pizza? When I am not prepared with some sort of plan for dinner.

When I not only have a plan but a freezer full of casseroles, soups, stews and the like, ready to be baked or simmered, I don't fall victim to getting takeout nearly as often, giving my budget a break. Not only that, but usually I can get some lunches to microwave at work from dinner leftovers.

If your college student stops in to visit you can sent your starving student back to the near-campus apartment with a frozen casserole or a big batch of chili, enough for your kid, the roommate and all their friends.

You are ready for a crazy day of work followed by soccer practice and piano lessons, knowing dinner will be waiting for you either in the ever-faithful Crock Pot or in a pre-programmed oven.

Know of a family with an illness or emergency? You're ready to come to their aid with a casserole from the freezer that they can heat and eat later.

Your kitchen stays cleaner because you're not in there cooking every night.

Best of all, when there's something for dinner already made, I can come home and relax, hang out with the kids, go for a run, enjoy a glass of wine, read a chapter of a book ... you name it. Meanwhile, dinner is in the oven. A bag of salad and rolls or garlic bread are all you need to make a complete meal.

Now the down side. You knew there was going to be a down side, right?

It is this: When you cook 30 meals in a day, you will be bone tired. Your back and feet and legs will hurt. You will smell like onions and sweat. Angry words will leave your lips, and your kitchen will look like a train wreck that involved marinara sauce and cream of mushroom soup.

There has to be a nice middle ground, one where you get your frozen assets while not knocking yourself out in the process. Here are a few ideas for how to get there:

Double up: When you make a batch of Poppyseed Chicken, Spaghetti Sauce, Taco Soup or Chili, make a little extra and freeze half of it. This is the most painless way of winding up with precooked dinners in your freezer.

The family plan: Those large family packs of ground beef and chicken can lend themselves to smaller cooking days. Think Spaghetti Sauce, Meat Loaf, beef for tacos and a pot of Chili, or making Chicken Tetrazzini, Chicken and Broccoli Rice and Poppyseed Chicken. For example, if you buy a five-pound package of ground beef, come up with recipes that together would call for five pounds of ground beef. Prepare and freeze and you are that much farther ahead on those busy weeknights.

Switch and swap: Get a few friends together and each of you take a recipe. Triple or quadruple it, depending on the number participating. Each of you make enough to feed your friends' families, packaging the dinners for freezing. Then swap. You may get there with four batches of Chili, but you would leave with Chili, Beef Lombardi, Chicken and Noodles and Chicken Enchiladas. It's four times easier to make one recipe than it is four.

And then there is Feed the Need.

Our group started at Madison United Methodist Church when Lee Ann Griffin had the idea of us meeting to cook together for an afternoon. Bulk cooking with groceries we all chipped in to pay for. It came to about $125 per family.

After about five hours, we all had about eight meals to take home for our families, plus loads more meals to donate to families who needed a good, hot, trouble-free meal.

I'm not going to pretend I have not been tired after cooking for an afternoon, but cooking with friends is a lot more enjoyable than cooking solo. Having friends to laugh and talk with makes cooking more fun and less tiring.

We also got to help others, some of whom were coping with crises and needed a good dinner.

And then there is coming home with the loot, eight or so meals! The servings were generous, too, meaning I had lunches and leftovers for later.

If I know I want to have Chicken Parmesan for dinner, for example, I just take the casserole out of the freezer either the night before or the morning of. Then that night, put the casserole in the oven, cook some Angel Hair pasta, warm some garlic bread and toss a salad. You're ready for company, if they're coming.

Those on the receiving end of our dinners get that same luxury of having dinner close to done after work. The time that they would otherwise be spending cooking can be spent with loved ones or just relaxing after a hard day.

There is also time and money saved by cooking ahead. You can get deals on ingredients purchased in bulk, and another plus is that you are in the supermarket less. Really, if you do this a lot, you may just be purchasing perishables, bread and produce.

That saves money, too, because rarely does our family stick to the grocery list. I have children, which means that someone is always going to want to have something extra at the supermarket. It doesn't take a genius to figure out that fewer trips to the store mean fewer impulse purchases.

Your kitchen stays cleaner, since you're not cooking every night, and if you use disposable aluminum containers and zippered plastic bags, you're not doing as many dishes. If I am cooking on a small scale at home and not cooking for the church freezer or to give to others, though, I like using my casserole dishes. To each her own.

Here are some of the recipes used. Try these out in your own home, or create your own cooking group and do the math to multiply the number of dinners.

Chicken Casserole
Cost $18
Prep and Cook Time 1 hour

8 chicken breasts
Salt
3 onions, chopped
2 bell peppers, chopped
8 ounces mushrooms
1 ½ sticks butter
1 pound angel hair pasta
3 cans Rotel tomatoes
¼ cup Worcestershire sauce
2 pounds Velveeta cheese

This makes two 9-inch-by13-inch casseroles.

Season chicken breasts with salt and boil until cooked. Remove chicken breasts; reserve 1 quart of the water. Let chicken cool, then chop or shred.

While chicken is cooking, sauté onions, peppers, and mushrooms in butter.

Cook pasta in the reserved chicken water until almost done. Add 3 cans Rotel, Worcestershire sauce, and sautéed veggies. Add in chicken and Velveeta; return to stovetop and heat until Velveeta has melted.

Pour into two 9-inch-by13-inch casserole dishes that have been sprayed with nonstick cooking spray.

Cover with aluminum foil and freeze. To cook, thaw by placing in refrigerator the night before you plan to serve. Bake at 350 until bubbly and heated through.

Chicken Parmesan Casserole
Cost $12

Prep Time 15 minutes / Bake 20-25 minutes

4 cups shredded, cooked chicken
1 jar marinara sauce
1 – 2 cups shredded mozzarella cheese
Salt and pepper, to taste

Layer chicken in bottom of casserole dish that has been sprayed with nonstick cooking spray. Pour in marinara sauce and mix with the chicken. Add salt and pepper. Top with cheese until all the chicken is covered. Cover with aluminum foil and freeze.

To bake, thaw completely by placing in refrigerator the night before you plan to serve. Bake at 350 for 20-25 minutes or until golden on top and bubbly on the sides. Serve with your favorite pasta or rice.

Spicy Pork Carnitas

Cost $10
Prep Time 5 minutes

Pork tenderloin
1 tsp. sea salt
1 Tbsp. Worcestershire sauce
2 tsp. cayenne pepper
2 cups apple cider vinegar
2 Tbsp. light soy sauce
2 tsp. hot sauce

Combine all ingredients in zippered plastic freezer bag and freeze.

To serve, thaw by placing in refrigerator the day before you plan to cook. Empty contents of bag into a Crock Pot and cook on low for eight hours. Shred meat and add to tacos or quesadillas.

Triple-Layer Taco Pie
Cost $15
Prep Time 30 minutes / Bake 30 minutes

2 cups cooked ground beef
1 can black beans, drained and rinsed
1 can diced tomatoes
1 cup corn
8 ounces cream cheese
2 Tbsp. sour cream
2 packets taco seasoning
3 flour tortillas
1 cup cheddar cheese

Cook and drain ground beef and prepare with one taco seasoning packet according to package directions. Beat cream cheese and sour cream with taco seasoning. Combine beans, diced tomatoes, corn, beef and cream cheese mixture until blended. Place one tortilla on the bottom of a pie pan that has been sprayed with nonstick cooking spray. Top with 1/3 of the above mixture. Repeat twice more and top with a tortilla. Sprinkle cheddar cheese on top. Cover with foil.

To prepare, thaw completely by placing in refrigerator the night before you plan to cook. Remove foil and bake at 350 until heated through, about 30 minutes.

Bacon-Swiss Burger Casserole
Cost $20
Prep Time 30 minutes / Bake 25-30 minutes

2 pounds ground chuck
1 cup chopped onion
1 can diced tomatoes, drained
1 cup ketchup
½ cup mayonnaise
1 Tbsp. Dijon mustard
1 ½ tsp salt
2 cups shredded Swiss cheese
2 cups shredded sharp cheddar cheese
1 (16 oz) package penne pasta, cooked and kept warm
For topping: 10 slices bacon (cooked and crumbled)

In a large skillet, combine ground chuck and chopped onion. Cook over medium heat until beef is browned and crumbly. Drain well. Add diced tomatoes, ketchup, mayo, mustard, and salt, stirring until combined. Stir in Swiss and cheddar cheeses.

Add penne pasta, stirring to combine. Spoon mixture into two 9-inch-by-13-inch pans that have been sprayed with nonstick cooking spray and cover with aluminum foil.

To prepare, thaw by placing in refrigerator the night before you plan to serve.

Bake at 350 for 25-30 minutes or until heated through.

Pizza Pasta Bake
Cost $20
Prep Time 15 minutes / Bake 20 minutes

1 pound penne, cooked and drained
1 cup Ricotta cheese
3 cups marinara sauce
30 – 40 slices pepperoni
½ cup sliced mushrooms
½ cup sliced black olives
2 cups shredded mozzarella cheese

Combine hot pasta with ricotta cheese and stir until cheese is melted and smooth. Pour into a 9-inch-by-13-inch pan that has been sprayed with nonstick cooking spray. Pour marinara sauce over the pasta. Top with pepperoni, mushrooms and olives. If you don't like mushrooms and black olives, omit those. Add shredded mozzarella cheese on top. Cover with foil and freeze.

To prepare, thaw by placing in refrigerator the night before you plan to bake. Bake at 350 for 20 minutes, or until warmed through and cheese is melted. Remove foil for the last half of cooking time.

Saucy Pizza Casserole
Cost $15
Prep Time 30 minutes / Bake 25-30 minutes

2 pounds ground beef
1 onion, chopped
2 28-ounce jars spaghetti sauce
16 ounces Rotini pasta
16 ounces shredded mozzarella cheese
5 ounces pepperoni

Brown ground beef and onion and drain. Set aside.
Meanwhile, boil rotini according to package directions and
drain. Place rotini in a large mixing bowl, and stir in meat,
onion and spaghetti sauce. Spray two 9-inch-by-13-inch
casserole dishes with nonstick cooking spray. Spread
noodle mixture in casserole dishes. Top each with
mozzarella cheese and pepperoni. Cover each dish with
aluminum foil and freeze.

To prepare, thaw a casserole by placing in refrigerator
the night before you plan to serve. Remove foil and bake
for 25-30 minutes at 350.

Vegetable Soup with Pasta
Cost $10
Prep Time 20 minutes / Bring to boil, simmer 15 minutes

1 pound ground chuck
½ cup chopped onion
½ tsp. dried oregano
2 (14.5 oz) cans stewed tomatoes, undrained
2 cups frozen mixed veggies
1 cup bowtie pasta (uncooked)
Salt and pepper

Brown the ground chuck and onion in large pot. Cook until the onion is tender. Drain grease. Add salt and pepper to taste.

Put meat/onion mixture in gallon zippered plastic freezer bag. Add tomatoes, veggies, uncooked pasta and oregano.

To prepare, thaw by placing in refrigerator the night before you plan to cook. To cook, pour into a large pot and bring to a boil. Reduce heat, cover and let simmer for 15 minutes or until pasta is tender. Serve hot, and pair it with cornbread and iced tea for a simple, satisfying meal.

Spaghetti Casserole
Cost $15
Prep Time 30 minutes / Bake 1 hour

1 package (16 ounces) Angel Hair pasta
1 1/2 pounds ground beef
1 jar (26 ounces) spaghetti sauce
2 cans (8 ounces each) tomato sauce (or 1 16 oz can)
1 can cream of mushroom soup
16 ounces sour cream
4 cups shredded Colby-Monterey Jack cheese

Cook pasta as directed on package. While pasta is cooking, brown beef in a large skillet and drain. Stir in spaghetti sauce and tomato sauce. Remove from heat.

In a separate bowl, stir together cream of mushroom soup and sour cream.

In two 9-inch-by-13-inch pans, layer half the meat sauce, pasta, sour cream mix and cheese. Repeat layers. Cover pans tightly with foil.

To prepare, thaw by placing in refrigerator the night before you plan to cook. Bake at 350 for about an hour.

Mexican Three-Bean Soup

Cost $15
Prep and Cook Time 1 hour

1 pound ground beef
1 diced onion
2 cans kidney beans
2 cans pinto beans
2 cans navy or Great Northern beans
1 can corn
1can stewed tomatoes
1can Rotel tomatoes with chilies
1 envelope taco seasoning mix
1 envelope ranch salad dressing mix

Brown beef and onion over medium heat. Drain. And undrained beans, corn, tomatoes and seasoning mixes. Simmer until flavors mix well (about 30 – 45 minutes). Let cool, then divide between two gallon-size zippered plastic freezer bags. Label and freeze flat, making sure to get as much air out of bags as possible before sealing.

To cook, thaw, then simmer on stove until heated through. Garnish with grated cheese and sour cream and serve with Fritos or tortilla chips, if desired.

Italian Chicken and Pasta Bake

Cost $15
Prep Time 1 hour / Bake 30-35 minutes

1 cup butter
1 cup chopped onion
4 cloves garlic, minced (or 1 Tablespoon minced garlic)
1/4 cup all-purpose flour
1 cup milk
2 cans diced tomatoes with basil, garlic and oregano
1 15-ounce can tomato sauce
3 cups chopped cooked chicken
4 cups shredded mozzarella cheese, divided
1 1/2 tsp. salt
1 tsp. ground black pepper
1/2 tsp. sugar
16 ounces bowtie pasta, cooked and kept warm

In a large skillet, melt butter over medium-high heat. Add onion and garlic, and cook for 5 to 6 minutes or until onion is tender. Add flour, and cook for 2 minutes, stirring constantly. Stir in milk, diced tomatoes, and tomato sauce; cook 5 to 6 minutes or until slightly thickened. Stir in chicken, 3 cups cheese, salt, pepper, and sugar. Stir in pasta. Spoon mixture into two 9-inch-by-13-inch casserole dishes that have been sprayed with nonstick cooking spray. Sprinkle remaining 1 cup cheese on top. Cover each dish with aluminum foil and freeze.

To serve, thaw overnight in refrigerator. Bake at 350 for 30-35 minutes or until hot and bubbly. Remove foil for the last 10 minutes of baking time.

Easy Freezer Chili
Cost $15
Prep and Cook Time 1 hour

2 pounds of ground beef
1 onion, chopped
3 cans chili beans
1 can Rotel tomatoes
1 can of diced tomatoes
2 envelopes chili seasoning
1/2 Tbsp. salt
2 cups water

Put browned ground beef into a pan with onions and cook until onions are soft. Add in all the other ingredients (including the juice of the tomatoes) and cook for 30 minutes or so until flavors have combined. Divide chili among three gallon-sized zippered plastic freezer bags, label and store flat in freezer, making sure to get as much air out of bags as possible before freezing.

To serve, thaw and simmer in pot until warm, or heat over a longer period of time in Crock Pot.

Easy Cheeseburger Casserole
Cost $15
Prep Time 45 minutes / Bake 25-30 minutes

For the topping:
2 pounds ground beef
1 onion
6 cups grated Cheddar cheese

For the crust:
5 cups self-rising flour or Bisquick
¾ cup sour cream
1 egg
1 cup water

Cook together the ground beef and onion over medium high heat until onion is soft. Set aside to cool.

Make the crust first by combining the flour or Bisquick, egg, sour cream and enough water to bring it together into a thick, but spreadable consistency.

Spray the pans with cooking spray and spread a layer of the dough into each one.

Sprinkle the cooled meat mixture over the dough, then top each one with about 2 cups of cheddar.

Cover each pan with aluminum foil and freeze. To prepare, thaw overnight in refrigerator. Bake at 350 for about 25-30 minutes or until cheese is bubbly and lightly browned.

Chicken and Broccoli Rice

Cost $20
Prep Time 1 hour / Bake 25-30 minutes

10 cups cooked rice
4 cups cooked chicken, chopped
4 cups chopped broccoli, lightly steamed (can use
  frozen or fresh)
2 cans cream of mushroom soup
2 cans cream of chicken soup
4 cups shredded cheddar cheese
Salt and pepper to taste

Combine all ingredients in a large bowl and mix well.
Divide between two 9-inch-by-13-inch pans that have been
sprayed with nonstick cooking spray, cover with
aluminum foil and freeze. To prepare, thaw overnight in
refrigerator. Sprinkle with additional shredded cheese, if
desired, and bake at 350 for 25-30 minutes or until heated
through and bubbly.

Chicken Tetrazzini

Cost $10
Prep Time 1 hour / Bake 30 minutes

1 can cream of mushroom soup
¾ cup water, or ½ cup water and ¼ cup white wine
½ cup Parmesan cheese, grated
¼ cup chopped green pepper, sautéed until tender
8 ounces Angel Hair pasta or spaghetti, cooked
   and drained
1 ½-2 cups boiled chicken, deboned, or use canned

In mixing bowl, blend all ingredients and pour into a casserole dish or aluminum pan that has been sprayed with nonstick cooking spray. Cover with foil and freeze. To heat, thaw overnight in refrigerator, top with grated cheddar cheese if desired and bake at 350 for about 30 minutes or until bubbly.

Baked Potato Soup

Cost less than $15
Prep and Cook Time less than 2 hours

10 pounds russet potatoes
1 cup butter
2 medium/large onions, chopped
2 Tbsp. minced garlic
2 tsp. salt
2 tsp. pepper
2 cups flour
12 cups chicken broth
4 cups half & half
1 pound sharp cheddar cheese, grated

Bake potatoes on a large baking sheet at 350 degrees for one hour, or until tender. Cool for about 15 minutes. Cut in half, and scoop flesh out into a large bowl. Melt butter in a large pot. Add onions and cook, stirring until soft, about 5 minutes. Add garlic, salt, pepper, and flour, stirring for another minute or so. Mixture will be pasty.

Gradually stir in broth, half & half, and then potatoes, and continue to heat, stirring every few minutes, until mixture has thickened, about 30 minutes. Don't let soup boil. Add cheese, and stir until melted. Let cool to room temperature, then divide among four gallon-sized zippered plastic freezer bags. Label, then freeze flat, making sure to get as much air as possible out of bags before sealing.

To prepare, thaw, then simmer on stove until heated through. Serve garnished with crumbled bacon or bacon bits, chopped green onions and shredded cheddar cheese.

Cheeseburger Soup

Cost less than $15
Prep and Cook Time 45 minutes

¾ cup chopped onion (about 1 medium)
1 tsp. dried parsley
1 Tbsp. butter
1 pound ground beef, browned and drained
2 cans low-sodium chicken broth
4 cups frozen, shredded hash browns, thawed
3 Tbsp. butter
¼ cup flour
1 ½ cups milk
2 cups cheddar cheese, shredded
¼ cup sour cream
Salt and pepper to taste

In a deep pan or Dutch oven, sauté onion and parsley flakes in 1 Tbsp. butter, until crisp-tender. Add broth, browned meat and potatoes to pan. Bring to a boil. Cover and simmer until potatoes are tender, about 10 minutes. Meanwhile, in a small skillet, melt 3 Tbsp. of butter and add ¼ cup of flour until a thick paste forms. Whisk in milk —about ½ cup at a time — and cook over medium heat until thickened, stirring frequently.

Add milk and flour mixture to soup, about ½ cup at a time, mixing in well. Bring to a boil and let boil about 2 minutes. Reduce heat to low. Add cheese and stir until cheese melts. Remove from heat and stir in sour cream. Add salt and pepper to taste. Freeze in gallon-sized zippered plastic freezer bags. To heat, thaw in refrigerator and heat by simmering on stove until heated through.

Istockphoto.com/sartorisliterary © warrengoldswain

7

Get Your Just Desserts

Dessert

Dessert is like a party waiting to happen.

Perhaps it is so much of a party that it influenced the direction of my life.

When I was a young girl, I would go with my mama to what my daddy referred to as "hen parties." Hen parties were great fun once I got past having to wear a dress and be on my best behavior. Dress-wearing and behaving has its privileges, though.

Dessert, namely.

There were petit fours and layer cakes at bridal showers and baby showers, which back in the day needed to be at least nine months apart to prevent town gossip. There were dump cakes and trifles at Mary Kay parties and Tupperware soirees. Just getting together for anything from coffee with the Daughters of the American Revolution to a Bible study usually had a brownie or a cookie involved.

And those were just the hen parties. Get the roosters involved, and we are talking dessert central. Church potluck buffet tables would be filled to capacity with banana puddings, caramel cakes, peach cobblers and pies, ranging from apple and sweet potato to lemon ice box and chocolate chess. Even family dinners had a dessert of some sort.

That was back in my girlhood during the 1970s. Since then, we're all gotten to be allergic to carbs and afraid of sugar.

Now, if you are out at a business lunch, it's nearly unheard of to say, "Why, yes, I believe I will have a slice of mile-high coconut pie."

Sweet tea can be a bit of an indulgence these days.

On dinner dates, if dessert is ordered, two spoons are involved, lest your date think you are a hog.

People look at you like you've got a substance abuse problem if you eat more than two brownies at a sitting.

This is unfortunate, because life should have a little sweetness. I recall having dinner out with one of my besties. We ate salad like we were being healthier than thou only to finish off dinner with pear tarts and wine.

Because life should be celebrated, and celebrations call for dessert. That and salad and dessert cancel each other out.

So back to how dessert directed the course of my life. Back in the day, in small-town Mississippi, a bridal shower, a particular type of hen party, was a particularly big deal. Such a big deal was this getting of toasters and coffee percolators that at one particular hen party that I was tagging along with mama to, a young woman with a camera arrived.

She immediately went to work, directing the bride-to-be and her mama and the groom's mama to stand together by the punch bowl and layer cake. A few snaps later, and she was chatting and eating cake with everyone else.

A couple of days later, the photo was in the daily newspaper. Turns out, the lady who visited the party was the newspaper's features editor, and back then, the newspaper covered hen parties.

That meant that this woman's job was going to parties. With dessert. This woman had what seemed to me at the time to be the coolest job ever. She got to be in print and be a professional dessert-eater and party-goer.

After thinking it over for maybe half a second, I decided I wanted a piece of that action.

Decades later, I turned out to be a features editor. I can tell you that there is a disturbing lack of dessert-eating and party-going in my job description.

'Nanner Puddin'
(Banana Pudding)
Cost $8
Prep Time 15 minutes, plus time to chill

I made this dessert for a gathering hosted by a deer-hunting colleague, Chris Todd. The Bambi Buffet had deer chili and deer sausage as its centerpiece, with the rest of us filling in with desserts and sides in the office potluck. I made this, a ridiculously good, creamy and cool dessert from my girlhood, and was told that, from there on out, I was required to bring it to every office potluck.

1 large box instant vanilla pudding
Milk
1 large container whipped topping, thawed
1 box vanilla wafers
4-5 bananas, peeled and sliced

Prepare pudding with milk according to package directions. To pudding, fold in about 2/3 of whipped topping. In casserole dish or 9-by-13-inch dish, layer vanilla wafers, bananas and pudding mixture until dish is filled. Place wafers around the edge of the dish, inserting the cookie's edge into the pudding. Top with remaining whipped topping and refrigerate before serving.

Strawberry Cake

Cost $8

Prep and Bake Time 1 hour

1 box white cake mix
1 cup oil
1 box strawberry Jell-O
4 eggs
1 package frozen strawberries
1 stick butter
1 pound powdered confectioner's sugar

This has been a girly birthday cake at our house more than once.

Preheat oven to 350. Spray 9-inch-by13-inch pan with nonstick cooking spray.

In large mixing bowl, combine cake mix, strawberry Jell-O and eggs.

Drain liquid from frozen strawberries and add enough water to make 1 cup liquid. Add juice and oil and mix thoroughly.

Bake in sprayed pan at 350 for 30-35 minutes.

For frosting, beat frozen berries, butter and confectioner's sugar. Frost cake once cooled.

Dream Cake

Cost $5

Prep and Bake Time 1 hour

This is such an easy cake to whip up, and it has been a hit at every tailgate party and church supper I have brought it to. The original recipe calls for yellow cake mix, but try it with chocolate cake mix, too.

1 box yellow cake mix
4 eggs
1 cup water
¾ cup oil
1 can coconut-pecan frosting

Preheat oven to 350. Spray Bundt pan liberally with nonstick cooking spray.

In large mixing bowl, combine all ingredients including the frosting and mix well.

Pour into Bundt pan and bake at 350 for 45 minutes or until cake is done.

Symphony Brownies
Serves 8-10
Cost $10
Prep and Bake Time 1 hour

2 boxes brownie mix, your favorite brand and type,
plus ingredients needed to prepare two batches
2 Symphony candy bars
Powdered confectioner's sugar

Prepare brownie mixes according to directions. Pour half of brownie batter into 9-inch-by 13-inch pan that has been sprayed with nonstick cooking spray. Take Symphony bars, which are milk chocolate bars with almonds and toffee, and break apart. Lay across top of brownie batter, and top this with second batch of brownie batter.

Bake according to brownie mix package directions.

These are decadent brownies, and I have taken them to an outdoor symphony concert, making them Symphony brownies on a whole new level.

Peach Cobbler
Cost $5
Prep and Bake Time 1 hour

This isn't the first recipe I ever tried for Peach Cobbler, but it is my favorite, for its ease as well as for the sweet bread on top. It will also make your house smell wonderful. If you're single, invite your beau over for this and he might just propose marriage.

1 stick butter or margarine (1/2 cup)
1 cup self-rising flour
1 cup milk
1 cup sugar
2 cups sliced peaches, fresh or canned

Preheat oven to 350. In your favorite 2-quart casserole dish, microwave stick of butter until melted. In mixing bowl, combine self-rising flour, sugar and milk. Pour this over melted butter. Pour peaches over batter. Bake for about 45 minutes or until crust has risen to the top and is golden brown.

Banana Split Cake

Cost $12

Prep Time 30 minutes, plus time to chill

1½ cups crushed graham crackers
1 cup sugar, divided
1/3 cup butter or margarine, melted
2 packages cream cheese, softened
1 20-ounce can crushed pineapple, drained
6 bananas
2 packages vanilla instant pudding
2 cups cold milk
2 cups whipped topping, thawed
1 cup chopped pecans

I first had this recipe when my friend Penny Porter Wilbourn's mom was hosting a Mary Kay party.

Mix graham cracker crumbs, ¼ cup sugar and melted butter in a small bowl. Pat into 9-inch-by-13-inch baking dish and freeze for about 10 minutes.

In large mixing bowl, beat cream cheese and ¾ cup sugar. Spread carefully over the graham cracker crust. Top this with drained crushed pineapple. Slice four bananas and put banana slices on top of pineapple layer.

In another large mixing bowl, beat pudding mixes and cold milk with a whisk. Fold in 1 cup whipped topping. Spread over banana layer.

Top with remaining whipped topping. Refrigerate several hours. Just before serving, slice remaining bananas and arrange on top of dessert. Top with chopped pecans, and garnish with Maraschino cherries, if desired.

Pecan Pie
Cost $10
Prep and Bake Time 1 hour

This is a recipe my mama used to make. We always have it with Thanksgiving dinner. One year, the middle son went shopping for Thanksgiving with me and said the Pecan Pie wasn't that important so I shouldn't make it. His older brother disagreed once we got home. We went back to the store for pecans and Karo.

> 1 frozen deep-dish pie crust (Make your own if you
>   want to be Martha Stewart)
> 2/3 cup sugar
> 1/3 cup butter or margarine, melted
> 1 cup Karo syrup, dark or light (Karo is a must!)
> ½ tsp. salt
> 3 eggs
> 1 cup pecan halves or pieces

Preheat oven to 375. In large mixing bowl, combine all ingredients, mixing with a whisk or an electric beater until well blended. Stir in pecans. Pour into pie crust that you have placed on a foil-lined baking sheet. Cover edges of pie crust to prevent it from becoming too brown. Bake about 40-50 minutes or until center is no longer jiggly. Take foil off crust after about 30 minutes. Let cool before serving, or make this the night before your dinner and refrigerate. Serve with whipped cream or whipped topping.

Sweet Potato Pie

Cost less than $8
Prep and Bake Time 1 hour

1 pound sweet potatoes
½ cup butter or margarine, softened
1 cup sugar
½ cup milk
2 eggs
½ tsp. nutmeg
½ tsp. cinnamon
1 tsp. vanilla extract
1 deep-dish pie crust

This is Southern comfort food, and a regular at holiday dinners. Make life easier and cook your sweet potatoes in the Crock Pot.

Bake sweet potatoes in Crock Pot 8 hours on low. You can also boil them whole in skins for about an hour. Either way, take out cooked potatoes and let them cool off.

Preheat oven at 350.

Cut open and scoop out sweet potato flesh and put into a large mixing bowl. Add butter, and mix well with electric mixer. Stir in sugar, milk, eggs, nutmeg, cinnamon and vanilla. Beat on medium speed until smooth.

Pour into unbaked pie crust. Bake for 1 hour or until knife inserted in center comes out clean. Serve with a dollop of whipped cream or whipped topping.

Lemon Ice Box Pie
Serves 8
Cost less than $8
Prep Time 15 minutes, plus time to chill

1 container of whipped topping
1/2 container of frozen lemonade or
  raspberry lemonade
1 can sweetened condensed milk
 1 graham cracker crust, ready-made, or use your
  favorite recipe

Combine half the frozen lemonade with sweetened condensed milk. Use rest of frozen lemonade to make half a batch of lemonade, or save for later in the freezer. Fold in whipped topping. Spoon into graham cracker crust. Place in refrigerator at least several hours to become firm. If desired, top with fresh strawberries or cherry pie filling.

This is an easy and luscious dessert perfect for a sweet ending to spring or summer dinners.

Birthday Ice Cream Cake
On the Cheap
Serves 6-8
Cost $10
Prep Time 15 minutes, plus time to freeze

12 ice cream sandwiches
1 large container of whipped topping, thawed
Chocolate syrup
Caramel or butterscotch ice cream topping
1-2 Butterfinger candy bars, crushed

This is a great recipe to get the kids involved with, as long as they don't eat all the ingredients.

Desserts you save money on without a lot of skill or hard work tend to taste better. Looking for ways to save on birthday parties, one summer we tried making our own ice cream cakes with great results. We haven't purchased a store-bought ice cream cake since.

The ice cream sandwiches in this dessert, when layered, give a torte-like appearance when the cake is cut. For our July birthday kids, we've grilled and served this as a sweet, cool treat, perfect for the summer when the last thing you want to do is heat up your kitchen by baking.

Here's how to make it: Unwrap ice cream sandwiches and place six of them in a 9-inch-by-13-inch pan or platter of your choice.

Frost liberally ith whipped topping. Drizzle with chocolate syrup and caramel topping. Sprinkle with half the crushed Butterfinger candy bars. (I crush them by putting the candy bars into a zippered plastic bag, sealing and crushing with a rolling pin.)

Pretend you are making lasagna and start over again with the other six ice cream sandwiches. Frost with the rest of the whipped topping, drizzle with chocolate syrup and caramel topping and sprinkle with the rest of the crushed candy bars.

Place in freezer until whipped topping is frozen and ice cream is firm. Sing "Happy Birthday," blow out any candles ablaze, slice and enjoy.

No-Guilt Coconut Cake

Cost less than $10
Prep and Bake Time 1 hour

1 box white cake mix
1 can Diet Sprite or Sprite Zero
½ cup fat-free sour cream
½ cup shredded coconut
½ cup Splenda
1 cup light whipped topping

Preheat oven to 350. Spray 9-inch-by-13-inch pan with nonstick cooking spray.

Mix cake mix and Sprite. Don't mix other ingredients called for on the cake mix box. Add coconut extract if you have it, but cake will be fine without it.

Bake according to cake mix package directions or until lightly golden brown.

While cake bakes, mix fat-free sour cream, Splenda and coconut. Reserve a few tablespoons of coconut for garnish if desired. Refrigerate.

Cool cake. Refrigerate overnight if possible.

Fold whipped topping into frosting. Frost the cooled cake and sprinkle with coconut.

Michael's Favorite Tea Cakes

Cost less than $4
Prep and Bake Time 1 hour

½ cup butter, softened
1 cup sugar
2 eggs
1 tsp. vanilla
2 ¾ cup flour
2 tsp. baking powder
½ tsp. salt

The youngest Dear Son loves these cookies!

Preheat oven to 350. Spray baking sheet lightly with nonstick cooking spray.

Cream butter and sugar with electric mixer until fluffy. Beat in eggs, and add vanilla. Stir flour, baking powder and salt together, and mix flour mixture into butter mixture. Drop by teaspoonfuls onto baking sheet.

Bake at 350 for 10-15 minutes or until cookies are golden brown.

Mini Cheesecakes
Makes 12
Cost $8
Prep and Bake Time 45 minutes

12 vanilla wafers
2 8-ounce blocks of cream cheese
½ cup sugar
1 tsp. vanilla
2 eggs
Cherry pie filling or blueberry pie filling

When helping host a progressive supper for our church's youth group, I came up with this recipe. A progressive supper, by the way, is when you serve each course at a different home. Our teenagers rode in the church van from the salad house to the entrée house to the dessert house, where this was waiting for them. I made several batches to feed the crew. They're especially good for a dessert buffet.

Preheat oven to 325. Line a muffin tin with foil liners. Paper ones will work but are not as pretty. Place one vanilla wafer in each muffin space.

With electric mixer, mix cream cheese, vanilla and sugar on medium speed until smooth. Add eggs. Mix well. Pour over wafers, filling ¾ full.

Bake for 25 minutes. Remove from oven and cool before removing from pan. To serve, top each with a spoonful of the pie filling of your choice.

Wacky Cake
Serves 6-8
Cost less than $5
Prep and Bake Time 45 minutes

1 ½ cups all-purpose flour
3 tbsp. cocoa, unsweetened
1 cup sugar
1 tsp. baking soda
½ tsp. salt
1 tsp. white vinegar
1 tsp. vanilla extract
5 tbsp. vegetable oil
1 cup water
Preheat oven to 350 degrees

This is the cake to make when you have more month than money. It's an oldie but a goodie, starting out as Depression Cake and then becoming Crazy Cake or Wacky Cake because of its odd list of ingredients, which doesn't include eggs but does include vinegar. Another wacky thing about this dessert is that it gets moister with time. It also is mixed in one pan, so fewer dishes to wash. No frosting is needed, but you can frost it if you like. A sprinkle of powdered sugar on top is enough sugar for us.

Spray an 8-inch baking pan with nonstick cooking spray. Mix dry ingredients in sprayed pan. Add vinegar, vanilla and oil. Pour water in, and mix with a spoon until smooth. Bake for 35 minutes or until done. Cool and then sprinkle with powdered sugar.

Chocolate Cobbler
Cost $4
Prep and Bake Time 1 hour

6 Tbsp. butter
1 cup self-rising flour
¾ cup sugar
1 ½ Tbsp. cocoa powder (Go with Hershey's – don't
substitute on this!)
½ cup milk
1 tsp. vanilla extract
1 cup sugar
¼ cup cocoa powder
1 ½ cups boiling water

Serve this with vanilla ice cream on top – it is nothing but decadent!

Preheat oven to 350. Melt butter in an 8-inch square baking dish while the oven preheats. In a medium-sized bowl, mix together flour, ¾ cup sugar and 1 ½ Tbsp. cocoa powder. Add milk and vanilla and stir until smooth. Spoon mixture over melted butter in baking dish.

Stir together remaining sugar and ¼ cup cocoa powder, Sprinkle on top of batter, and pour 1 ½ cups boiling water over top.

Bake for 30 minutes or until set. Cool slightly, serving when still warm.

Chocolate Lasagna

Cost $8
Prep Time 30 minutes, plus time to chill

**1 box Oreo cookies, crushed (A neat way to do this is
to put them in a zippered plastic bag, sealed, and
roll over them with your handy, dandy rolling
pin. Work out any frustration or stress.)**
6 Tbsp. margarine or butter
**8 ounces cream cheese, regular or reduced
fat, softened**
¼ cup sugar
1 container refrigerated whipped topping, thawed
2 boxes instant chocolate pudding
Milk
Mini chocolate chips
Gummy worms if you are making this for kids

This can also be done in individual cups or bowls,
and, if garnished with a gummy worm, it can be Dirt and
Worms, one of my kids' favorite desserts in their younger
days.

Place crushed Oreo cookies in a large mixing bowl.
Melt butter or margarine and add to cookie crumbs,
mixing to blend. Mash buttered crumbs into the bottom of
a 9-inch-by-13-inch pan that has been sprayed with
nonstick cooking spray. Put cookie crust in refrigerator
while you work on other layers.

With electric mixer, beat cream cheese until fluffy,
adding in sugar and 2 Tbsp. milk. Fold in about 1 ½ cups

refrigerated whipped topping. Spread this over the cookie crust.

Empty pudding mix into a mixing bowl and add milk as directed on package, whisking to blend. Let sit for 5-10 minutes to become firm.

Spoon this over the cream cheese layer.

Spoon the rest of your refrigerated whipped topping over the chocolate pudding layer, and sprinkle with mini chocolate chips. If you are making Dirt and Worms, reserve some of the Oreo crumbs to go on top to make it more dirt-like.

Refrigerate for several hours before serving.

Husband's Delight

Cost $8

Prep Time 45 minutes

Since I don't have one of those at the time of this writing, Husband's Delight is an odd recipe for me to include, but a girl can hope. Whether you're married or single, this is delicious.

1 ¼ cup flour
½ cup chopped pecans
1 stick butter or margarine

Preheat oven to 325. Mix ingredients, pat into a 9-inch-by-13-inch dish and bake for 20 minutes. Let cool.

8 ounces cream cheese, regular or reduced fat, softened
1 cup confectioner's sugar
½ cup refrigerated whipped topping, thawed

With electric mixer, beat cream cheese and sugar until fluffy. Fold in refrigerated whipped topping. Spoon this over cooled crust. Refrigerate.

2 packages of your favorite instant pudding
3 cups milk

In mixing bowl, whisk together pudding and milk until blended. Let set for 5-10 minutes to firm. Spoon this over cream cheese layer. Top with the rest of refrigerated whipped topping, and sprinkle chopped pecans over top if desired. Refrigerate for several hours before serving.

8

Breakfasts:
Rise and Shine

Breakfast is Served

It's the most important meal of the day

I don't get people who don't like eating breakfast. I have children who, some days, are not in the mood for food first thing in the morning.

This doesn't make sense to me, because I am hungry enough to gnaw on a table leg when my feet hit the floor.

"Breakfast" means breaking the fast, since you haven't eaten since the night before. You should be hungry. Eight hours is a long time.

Plus there are so many delicious options. Bacon is a breakfast food. So is sausage. There are eggs any way you can cook them. Smoothies. Muffins. Biscuits. Bagels. Cereal. Fruit. Yogurt.

We love weekends, and really, who doesn't? One of the ways we celebrate a couple of days when we don't have to run off to work and school is by having big, leisurely breakfasts.

Saturdays, we usually have bacon and eggs or Cheese Omelets, biscuits or toast, and I treat myself to a few cups of coffee, either French roast with a sprinkle of cinnamon in the grounds or hazelnut. My sweet babies often give me gourmet flavored coffees as gifts, and they are always enjoyed.

Saturday mornings, before anyone else is up, I like to go outside and relax in the Adirondack chair the Gentleman Friend built for me. I take with me a plate of a savory breakfast, a hot cup of coffee and the family dog, who keeps the squirrels at bay. I also bring along a good book, usually something on the inspirational side.

And I eat, read, sip coffee and relax, knowing I don't have to rush off anywhere.

The breakfast fest continues into Sunday, when we continue what is a family tradition. I don't know how far back it goes, but my mother did it, and I do it now. Maybe it goes back to my grandmother or great-grandmother. I like to think that it does.

The Sunday breakfast tradition is bacon or sausage plus pancakes or waffles, followed by church.

Sometimes they're blueberry pancakes, or oatmeal pancakes, but usually they are the regular kind, either made from scratch, a mix or Bisquick, with butter and syrup.

I'm not sure why the tradition started. Maybe it was to keep everyone full and happy during church services. Maybe it was to remind the family that Sunday is a day of sweetness. Or maybe it was a good way to get the family together.

But just about every Sunday I can remember during my growing-up years, we had pancakes on Sunday. My children have pancakes on Sunday, too.

Breakfast, as it turns out, not only feeds the body, but the spirit, too.

Rise and shine.

Biscuits

One of the first things I learned to cook as a teenager was a biscuit. I am not talking about what I refer to as a "thwack" biscuit, the kind that comes in a can that you "thwack" on the kitchen counter to open. No, these were scratch biscuits, and Mrs. Mary Ruth Hill didn't see why any self-respecting woman wouldn't whip up a pan of these every morning.

I will confess a few things. One is that when I make homemade biscuits, I feel like a better mama. A little butter and some strawberry preserves or honey makes these into something from heaven.

Another is that I take shortcuts. I don't use all-purpose flour and add in the baking powder and salt and then cut in the shortening. No, I am a Bisquick girl. Bisquick is truly a convenience food.

I like rolled biscuits cut with my mama's biscuit cutter, but drop biscuits are good in a pinch. Do it the way you like.

2 ¼ cups Bisquick, regular or heart healthy
2/3 cup milk

Heat oven to 450. Mix Bisquick and milk together, and turn onto a Bisquick-powdered pastry cloth. Trust me, you need one of those. Pastry cloths make life so much easier. Fold dough over again and again when kneading, mashing down each time. This gives you nice layers in your biscuits. Roll out about ½ inch thick. Cut into biscuits, place on a nonstick baking sheet and bake at 450 for about 8 minutes or until golden brown.

If you're making drop biscuits, skip the kneading and drop by tablespoonfuls onto your baking sheet.

Fun with Dough

Now you have biscuit dough. There is no limit to the fun you can have. Oh, wait, there is a limit. It's called "your imagination."

Cinnamon rolls: Roll out dough on a flour-covered pastry cloth. Brush with melted butter or margarine, Sprinkle with white or brown sugar blended with about ½ tsp. to 1 tsp. cinnamon. Roll up and slice. Place in a muffin tin that has been sprayed with nonstick cooking spray. Bake at 450 for about 8 minutes.

Cheese pinwheels: Roll out dough on a flour-covered pastry cloth. Sprinkle with your favorite shredded cheese blend. Roll up and slice. Place on a baking sheet and bake at 450 for 8 minutes.

Pigs in blankets: Wrap a strip of biscuit dough around a little smoked cocktail wienie. Repeat a bunch of times.

Biscuit muffins: Roll dough into two or three balls per muffin space. Dip each ball into melted butter. Place two or three balls into each muffin space, making sure your muffin pan has been sprayed with nonstick cooking spray. You can sprinkle with cinnamon sugar if you'd like. Bake at 450 for 8-10 minutes or until golden brown.

Cheddar-Sausage Muffins
Makes 48 mini muffins
Cost $7
Prep and Bake Time 1 hour

1 pound bulk pork sausage, hot or mild
1 can cheddar cheese soup
½ cup water
3 cups Bisquick

Preheat oven to 400. Spray mini muffin tins with nonstick cooking spray.

Crumble sausage and brown over low to medium heat. Drain.

In mixing bowl, combine sausage, cheddar cheese soup and water. Add Bisquick and stir to combine.

Spoon batter into mini muffin tins and bake for 10-15 minutes or until golden brown.

Angel Biscuits
Cost $5
Prep and Bake Time 30 minutes

5 cups flour
1 cup shortening
5 tsp. baking powder
1 tsp. salt
3 tsp. sugar
1 envelope yeast
2 cups buttermilk
2 Tbsp. warm water

I've also seen these called "Brides' Biscuits" because they're a kitchen shortcut that doesn't taste like one. The taste and appearance looks like you slaved away in the wee hours of the morning, when in reality, you had the dough already sitting in your fridge.

Preheat oven to 450.

In a small bowl, dissolve yeast in warm water and set aside. Sift together dry ingredients and place in large mixing bowl. Cut in shortening. Add buttermilk and yeast. On flour-covered pastry cloth, knead dough lightly. Do not let rise. On pastry cloth, roll out desired amount of dough. Cut out into biscuits and bake for about 8 minutes.

Store the rest of dough in a covered plastic container. It will keep for about a month, but trust me, you'll use it up before then. Just roll out, cut and bake when you're ready for biscuits.

Friendship Bread

Cost $8
Prep and Bake Time 1 hour

I had a co-worker who gave me the starter for this bread, and it is yummy. My children have loved this cinnamon-y bread at breakfast or any time. It's also really good with a mug of herbal tea as an evening snack.

Starter:
¼ cup warm water
1 envelope active dry yeast
1 cup sugar
1 cup flour
1 cup warm milk
4 gallon-size zippered plastic bags

In a glass measuring cup, add ¼ cup warm water and yeast, allowing yeast to dissolve. Stir and set aside.

In plastic or glass bowl, combine sugar and flour with a wire whisk. Slowly stir in milk and then yeast mixture. Stir until blended.

Consider this the first day of the 10-day cycle. Cover loosely and let set at room temperature. If storing in a zippered plastic bag, occasionally let the air out.

Days 2-5: Mash bag to mix.

Day 6: Add to bag 1 cup flour, 1 cup sugar and 1 cup milk. Mash bag to blend.

Days 7-9: Mash bag to mix.

On the tenth day, take three other zippered plastic bags, and into each bag, pour in 1 cup starter. Keep one bag and give three to your friends.

Bread:
1 cup live starter
1 cup oil
½ cup milk
3 eggs
1 tsp. vanilla extract
2 cups flour
1 cup sugar
1 ½ tsp. baking powder
2 tsp. cinnamon
½ tsp. baking soda
1 small box instant vanilla pudding
½ tsp. salt
1 cup chopped pecans (optional)

Preheat oven to 325. In a medium-sized mixing bowl, combine wet ingredients and stir until eggs are beaten and mixture is well blended. In a large mixing bowl, stir together dry ingredients, and then add wet mixture and stir until well blended. Bake for 1 hour.

Bran Muffins

Cost $8
Prep and Bake Time 30 minutes

4 eggs
3 cups sugar
1 quart buttermilk
6 cups bran cereal, with or without raisins
5 cups flour
1 cup oil
5 tsp. baking soda
1 tsp. salt

I will warn you that this isn't the prettiest batter in the world, but it will keep for about six weeks in the refrigerator, meaning you are just minutes from warm, fresh muffins. These are also a delicious way to get your fiber.

In largest mixing bowl you have, beat eggs and sugar until well blended. Stir in buttermilk, cereal, flour, oil, baking soda and salt. Stir well. Keep in large covered plastic container. Refrigerate at least six hours before using.

To make muffins, preheat oven to 400. Spray a muffin pan with nonstick cooking spray or use paper liners. Fill muffin cups about two-thirds full, and bake for 15-20 minutes or until muffins are done.

Monkey Bread
Cost $7
Prep and Bake Time 45 minutes

One time, I was out writing about wedding trends and how couples are ditching tradition and making their nuptials more personal. A caterer with a booth at a wedding show said one groom didn't want wedding cake. He wanted monkey bread. I totally get that, because monkey bread is delicious. It makes a decadent Saturday morning breakfast, and for one happy couple, a wedding cake replacement.

4 cans refrigerated biscuits
2/3 cup sugar
2 tsp. cinnamon
1 ¼ sticks butter or margarine
cup brown sugar

Preheat oven to 350. Spray Bundt pan with nonstick cooking spray.

Cut biscuits in half. Pour sugar and 1 tsp. cinnamon into a plastic bag. Put a few biscuits at a time into the bag and shake. Arrange shaken biscuits in Bundt pan.

Melt butter, brown sugar and cinnamon in saucepan and pour over biscuits.

Bake for 30 minutes or until done.

Real Men *Do* Eat Quiche
Cost $10
Prep and Bake Time 1 hour

This is one quiche that men love! Sausage, cheese … lots of manly ingredients! And the sour cream really gives it a sinful flavor. This never sticks around long at our house.

> ½ pound bulk pork sausage, hot or mild
> 6 eggs
> 1 unbaked pie crust
> ½ cup sour cream
> Salt
> Pepper
> 1 pound cheddar cheese, shredded, or cheese blend
> Parsley

Preheat oven to 350. Crumble and brown sausage and drain. Beat eggs well. Whisk in sour cream along with salt and pepper to taste.

Sprinkle sausage into pie crust. Top with cheese. Pour egg mixture over all. Sprinkle with parsley.

Bake 35-45 minutes or until golden brown and filling is set.

Sausage Pinwheels
Makes about 24 Pinwheels
Cost $5
Prep and Bake Time 30 minutes

**1 pound bulk pork breakfast sausage, hot or mild
(we like hot)**
2 rolls of refrigerated crescent roll dough

Once upon a Christmas morning, I made these after a friend told me the recipe. It's that simple, something that can be remembered without writing it down. The next year, I didn't make these, and you'd have thought I had desecrated the home, family, Christmas and Baby Jesus. Since then, they've been a staple for holiday mornings, but they're delicious anytime. Serve them up with hot coffee and orange juice.

Preheat oven to 375. On a cutting board or baking sheet, roll out triangles of dough from one of the containers and mash together the edges until you have a rectangle of dough. Take half of raw sausage and smooth over rectangle of dough. Roll up as if you were making cinnamon rolls or a jelly roll. Slice into pieces about ½ inch thick and place on baking sheet. Bake according to crescent roll dough package directions until rolls are golden brown and sausage is cooked. Repeat with other half of dough and sausage.

Pigs in Blankets
Makes Eight Pigs in Blankets
Cost $6
Prep and Bake Time 30 minutes

Eight link breakfast sausages
1 container refrigerated crescent roll dough

These are quick, easy and will bring your family running to the breakfast table.

Preheat oven to 375. Cook and drain sausages. Open dough and roll each triangle of dough around a sausage. Place on baking sheet and bake according to refrigerated crescent roll dough directions or until golden brown.

Breakfast Burritos

Cost $7
Prep and Cooking Time 30 minutes

These are just delicious. Make these and you'll turn your nose up at the fast-food kind! They're also great to take with you if you have a busy weekend, say, a baseball or soccer practice to take the kids to, errands or what have you.

½ pound bulk pork sausage, hot or mild
1 Tbsp. taco seasoning, or about half an envelope
6 eggs
½ cup shredded Mexican four-cheese blend
4 flour tortillas
Salsa

Brown sausage and taco seasoning in skillet and drain. Add sausage back to skillet and add the eggs, beaten, and let cook on medium until eggs begin to set. Scramble until eggs are done, but still moist. Spoon mixture into warm tortillas (Microwave for about 15-20 seconds) and top with cheese and salsa. Roll as a burrito.

Cheese Omelets
Serves 1-2
Cost $2
Prep and Cooking Time 10 minutes

2-3 eggs
Salt and pepper
Water
½ cup shredded cheese (I like the blends, such
   as Mexican four-cheese or cheddar and pepper jack)

Spray a small skillet liberally with nonstick cooking spray. Put small skillet on medium heat. In a mixing bowl, crack eggs and season with salt and pepper to taste. Add about 3 Tbsp. water, and, with a wire whisk, beat egg mixture thoroughly. Pour mixture into skillet.

A note on the water: It makes for a lighter omelet, as the water turns to steam as it cooks. Here comes the tricky part: As the eggs cook, pierce bubbles that form, letting the egg liquid flow underneath. Slightly lift edges of the omelet, to get more liquid underneath. Keep doing this until the top of the omelet is no longer liquid-y. Sprinkle with cheese and carefully fold omelet in half.

Here is when that nonstick cooking spray becomes very important: Flip omelet out of skillet and onto a plate. Serve up, either to yourself or share. This is a tricky recipe that takes some practice to perfect. Don't worry if you mess it up – you can always declare the recipe "scrambled eggs," and it will still eat good.

Breakfast Sausage Casserole
Cost $8
Prep and Cooking Time 1 hour

6 slices bread, crusts removed
1 tsp. dry mustard
1 tsp. salt
2 cups half and half
¼ cup butter or margarine
1 ½ cup shredded cheddar cheese
1 pound bulk pork breakfast sausage, hot or mild
   (we like the hot!)
5 eggs, well beaten

I remember being served this during my high school years, usually at brunches for graduating seniors. Pair it up with fresh fruit and muffins, and it's still a brunch-worthy choice. Another plus, one I didn't realize as a high-schooler, is that it is made the day before. That makes it a nice option for Christmas morning, or any day you need to skip a little prep work in the morning.

Cook sausage in skillet until done, and drain off any grease. Melt butter or margarine and pour into a 9-inch-by-13-inch baking dish. Tear bread into small pieces and place over butter. Sprinkle crumbled cooked sausage over bread, and then sprinkle shredded cheddar cheese over sausage. Beat eggs and remaining ingredients. Pour over cheese. Cover with plastic wrap and refrigerate overnight, or eight hours. Bake at 350 for 40-50 minutes.

Donis' Bacon Egg Cups

Cost Less than $5
Prep and Bake Time 30 minutes

I have been privileged to teach teenagers in Sunday school with Donis Upshaw. I get as much out of her lessons as the kids do, plus she shared this recipe with me, which is yummy to have before church. You may want to bake this on top of a baking sheet as the cups do like to overflow a little.

1 can refrigerated biscuits
3 eggs
3 Tbsp. milk
4 slices bacon, cooked and crumbled
½ cup shredded cheese
Salt and pepper

Preheat oven to 400. Spray muffin pan with nonstick cooking spray. In mixing bowl, whisk eggs and milk together. Season with salt and pepper and set aside.

Roll out biscuits until they are a little larger than the muffin cups. Press a biscuit into each cup.

Sprinkle cheese into each cup.

Pour egg into each cup, only filling half full. Even at half full, you might have some overflowing going on as the biscuit dough rises. Sprinkle with bacon pieces.

Bake for 10-12 minutes or until biscuit dough is done and eggs are set. Loosen from muffin pan with a butter knife and serve warm.

Blueberry Muffins

Cost $4

Prep and Bake Time 30 minutes

1 ½ cups flour
¾ cup sugar
½ tsp. salt
2 tsp. baking powder
½ cup vegetable oil
1 egg
1/3 cup milk
1 cup blueberries

When our family lived in West Point, Mississippi, there was a blueberry farm we visited in Lowndes County, and my two oldest sons and I had the best time. We picked fat blueberries, the kids eating just about as many as they picked. We took them home and prepared them for freezing: We spread the unwashed berries (water makes them tough) on a baking sheet and froze them, then stored them in a zippered plastic freezer bag. When ready to use, measure out the needed quantity and wash in a colander.

Preheat oven to 400.

Spray muffin pan with nonstick cooking spray.

In large mixing bowl, combine flour, sugar, salt and baking powder. Stir in egg, oil and milk. Stir until lumpy, but don't overmix.

Fold in rinsed blueberries. Fill muffin pan. Bake for 20-25 minutes or until muffins are done.

Banana Bread

Cost $7
Prep and Bake Time 1 hour

2 very ripe bananas, mashed
2/3 cup sugar
¼ cup milk
3 Tbsp. vegetable oil
½ tsp. vanilla extract
3 eggs
2 2/3 cups Bisquick baking mix
½ cup chopped pecans

This is the recipe to make when you find overripe bananas on sale at the supermarket, because you want to use very ripe bananas for baking. They're much sweeter.

Preheat oven to 350.

Spray loaf pan with nonstick cooking spray.

Stir bananas, sugar, milk, oil, vanilla and eggs in large mixing bowl. Stir in Bisquick and nuts. Pour into pan.

Bake for about an hour or until toothpick inserted in center comes out clean. Cool before removing from pan.

Strawberry Smoothies
Cost $3
Prep Time 10 minutes

Be healthier than thou with these. They're also yummy, so your kids will drink them!

1 container strawberry fat-free yogurt
1 ½ cups skim milk
1 cup strawberries, fresh or frozen
1 banana, sliced

Put all ingredients in a blender and blend on high until smooth. I have also made this with a food processor with good results.

Pour into two glasses and serve immediately.

9

Rabbit Food: Salads and Lighter Fare

Salad Days

Shakespeare referred to them.

H.I. McDonough referred to them.

Salad days. A time of youthful indiscretion, or if that sounds too naughty, how about a time of carefree life. In "Anthony and Cleopatra," Shakespeare had the heroine looking back on her "salad days" when she was green in judgment.

Mr. McDonough, in Joel and Ethan Coen's "Raising Arizona," was talking of he and wife Ed's early days of marriage as their "salad days."

How odd it is that salad days can mean a time of fun and perhaps frivolity but when we're really eating salads, it is either a time of January dieting or dealing with triple-digit summer temperatures.

When I was a girl, salad time was when the window air conditioner could barely take the edge off the heat and my mama couldn't bare to heat up the kitchen. Daddy and I couldn't bare to eat anything above room temperature, so salads were appealing.

Salad days for me now are the times when I am doing penance for overindulging, usually over the holiday season. They're not carefree. They are intentional days of kale-eating in an attempt to hold back calories and fit into my skinny jeans.

Cleopatra referring to salad days and green judgment strikes me as ironic, since my green judgment is usually prior to my salad days, and usually the reason I'm eating kale to begin with.

Salad, I believe, has magical calorie-removing properties. Something delicious and indulgent, such as Fettucine Alfredo or a cheese-loaded square of lasagna, seems less of a bad diet choice if it is accompanied by a big salad glistening with vinaigrette.

If the road to diet hell is paved with good intentions, then salads are where we go astray.

Salads sound so healthier than thou, but some salads, the ones topped with bacon, cheese, creamy dressings and the like, can be more than 1,000 calories. You might as well top that lettuce with chocolate cake.

Salads, and what used to be called a cold plate in the ice box, a sampling of salads ranging from potato salad to chicken salad to concoctions from aspic to fruit to pasta, are a staple of Southern life. I look forward to a salad lunch with friends, perhaps our Mississippi University for Women alumni lunch bunch, where I get the modern version of a cold plate served up with a tall glass of iced tea.

We may be more practical than green when we're choosing what to eat during our salad days, but few things can get you through January or July like a salad.

Sunshine Salad

Cost less than $4
Prep Time 30 minutes, plus time to chill

1 small box lemon Jell-O
1 cup boiling water
1 8-ounce can crushed pineapple
2 Tbsp. lemon juice or vinegar
2-3 carrots, peeled and finely grated
Mayonnaise or Miracle Whip (optional)

This is a 1950s-era Jell-O Salad we learned to make in high school home economics. I remember thinking at the time that carrots would be nasty in Jell-O, but then I tried our class assignment and stood corrected.

Drain pineapple, reserving juice. Set pineapple aside. Pour pineapple juice into a measuring cut and add lemon juice or vinegar. Add enough cold water to equal 1 cup. Dissolve Jell-O in 1 cup boiling water. Stir pineapple and carrots into gelatin with reserved juice blend. Pour into 8-inch square baking dish or into your favorite Jell-O mold, if you're getting fancy.

Or if you have them, use the little individual Jell-O molds. I got a nice set of them at a yard sale. Refrigerate until set. Unmold or cut into squares, depending on your choice of dish or mold. Top each serving with a dollop of mayonnaise or Miracle Whip if desired.

Taco Salad
Cost $12
Prep Time 30 minutes

1 pound lean ground beef
1 envelope taco seasoning
1 head Iceberg lettuce
1 can kidney beans, drained
1 ½ cup cheddar cheese, grated
1 tomato, chopped
½ red onion, chopped
Crushed Doritos to taste
Catalina salad dressing, to taste

Brown ground beef in a skillet, crumbling the meat as it cooks. Drain fat. Add taco seasoning with ¾ cup water and follow package directions. Set aside to allow meat to cool while you prepare the rest of the salad. Rinse and tear Iceberg lettuce into bite-sized pieces. Toss with drained beans, chopped tomato, chopped red onion and grated cheese. Toss in seasoned beef. Crumble Doritos and sprinkle on salad, and toss with Catalina dressing. Serve on plates or in salad bowls. This is a sweet yet tangy salad that's a nice light meal for a hot day.

Candy Apple Salad
Cost $10
Prep Time 30 minute

Only in the South would someone create a recipe
calling for pudding mix and chopped Snickers bars and
call it a salad. But this is quite good. Try it for dessert,
though.

1 ½ cups milk
1 small box instant vanilla pudding
1 small container whipped topping (Cool Whip)
4-6 Granny Smith apples, cored and chopped, or mix
  Granny Smiths and Fuji apples for a color mix
Lemon juice
4 Snickers bars, chopped

In a large bowl, whisk together milk and pudding mix
for 2 minutes, and let stand until pudding is soft set, about
2 minutes. Fold in whipped topping. Squeeze enough
lemon juice on apples to prevent them from browning.
Fold in chopped apples and chopped candy bars.
Refrigerate until serving.

Fluff Salad

Cost $6
Prep Time 5 minutes, plus time to chill

This is easy, creamy and so good on a hot day. It may be a salad, but I like having it as a dessert.

1 small can crushed pineapple
1 small box of Jell-O, any flavor, although lime and
    raspberry flavors are especially good
1 1/2 cups cottage cheese
1 small container frozen whipped topping
    (Cool Whip), thawed

In serving dish or bowl, pour in pineapple, undrained. Add Jell-O powder and stir to combine. Add cottage cheese and combine. Fold in Cool Whip and refrigerate for several hours. This is an easy salad to put together in the morning before work, and it's ready to serve when you get back home.

Pistachio Salad

Cost $5
Prep Time 5 minutes, plus time to chill

And what Southern salad collection is complete without a recipe that includes pudding mix and marshmallows? You can have this for dessert if you'd rather.

2 cups mini marshmallows
14 ounces crushed pineapple
1 box pistachio pudding mix
1 carton whipped topping

Fold all ingredients together in a large bowl. Refrigerate until chilled.

Pear Salad

Cost $3
Prep Time 5-10 minutes

1 can pear halves, in heavy or light syrup, drained
Mayonnaise, regular or light, or salad dressing such as
Miracle Whip
Finely shredded cheddar cheese

When I was a girl, we'd go out to eat usually once a week and almost always Sunday noon after church. We'd only hope the preacher wouldn't get long-winded since that would mean the Methodists and Presbyterians would beat us Southern Baptists to the buffet line at the Southern Inn. Often these salads would be on buffets, and they were always a favorite for their sweet but tangy flavor. They're also inexpensive and easy to make at home.

Set drained pear halves cut side up on a serving plate, or place on individual salad plates. These are especially pretty on top of lettuce leaves. Spoon about a teaspoon of mayonnaise on top of each pear half and sprinkle with shredded cheddar cheese. Refrigerate covered to prevent cheese from drying out.

Peach Salad

Cost $4
Prep Time 5-10 minutes

This is like a first cousin to the Pear Salad, and is just as pretty. Like quite a few other Southern salad ideas, Peach Salads are a nice, light dessert option.

1 can peach halves, in heavy or light syrup, drained
Cottage cheese
Maraschino cherries

Arrange drained peach halves on a serving platter or on individual salad plates. These are also pretty atop lettuce leaves. You can tell if these are a salad or dessert this way: Lettuce leaves signal it's a salad.

Top each peach half with a generous dollop or scoop, if you're getting fancy, of cottage cheese. Top each salad serving with a maraschino cherry. Refrigerate until you're ready to serve.

Fruit salad

Cost $8
Prep Time 5-10 minutes

1 can peach pie filling
2-3 bananas, sliced
1 can mandarin oranges, drained
1 can sliced pears, drained
1 container frozen strawberries, thawed and
  drained, or use fresh

One Christmas Eve, the Oeth family had breakfast for dinner: Ham, quiche, biscuits, cheese grits, store-bought coffee cake and this lovely fruit salad. It's bright, delicious and doesn't depend on fruits in season, so you can enjoy this any time of the year.

Fold fruits together in your favorite salad bowl or serving dish and refrigerate until serving. If you are making this ahead of time, slice and add bananas at the last minute to prevent browning.

Spinach Salad with Strawberries
Cost less than $10
Prep Time 15 minutes

Fresh spinach or baby spinach
1 container fresh strawberries, washed and halved
1 cup pecan pieces, tossed with cinnamon sugar and
**   a small amount of margarine and butter, and toasted**
Poppyseed salad dressing

Wash spinach and tear into bite-sized pieces as
needed. Add strawberries. Add toasted cinnamon sugared
pecans. Toss with poppy seed dressing just before serving.

Broccoli Salad

Cost $5
Prep Time 30 minutes

2 bunches fresh broccoli, cut into flowerets
1 cup sunflower seeds
1 cup raisins
1 bunch green onions, chopped
1 cup grated cheddar cheese
1 pound bacon, fried crisp and crumbled
Mayonnaise, regular or light, or Miracle Whip

Combine ingredients and toss together in your favorite salad bowl or serving dish. Combine with mayonnaise to taste.

Tomatoes and Cucumbers
Cost $5
Prep Time 15 minutes

Tomatoes, sliced and halved or quartered, depending on desired size
Cucumbers, sliced
Salt
Pepper
Extra virgin olive oil or your favorite vinaigrette or Italian dressing

I love growing these two veggies in our garden, and they pair up so nicely for a quick and easy salad.

Combine vegetables in your favorite salad bowl or serving dish. Season to taste with salt and pepper. Drizzle with extra virgin olive oil, vinaigrette or Italian salad dressing and refrigerate.

Cucumber Salad, Two Ways
Cost $4
Prep Time 10 minutes

If you have cucumbers growing in your garden, you know they can be quite prolific some years. Here are two ways to use them up.

Option 1:
Mayonnaise Cucumber Salad

Cucumbers, peeled and sliced
Salt
Pepper
Mayonnaise or Miracle Whip

Place cucumbers in your favorite salad bowl or serving dish. Sprinkle with salt and pepper to taste. Add mayonnaise to your preference and blend. Refrigerate. As salad chills, mayonnaise thins as it combines with juice from cucumbers.

Option 2:
Sweet and Sour Cucumber Salad

Cucumbers, peeled and sliced
Salt
Pepper
Sugar
Vinegar
Oil

Place cucumbers in your favorite salad bowl or serving dish. Sprinkle with salt and pepper to taste. In small bowl, combine 2-3 Tbsp. of oil and 1-2 Tbsp. of vinegar plus 1 Tbsp. sugar to make dressing and toss with cucumbers. Make this salad ahead of time as it needs time to refrigerate and for flavors to blend.

Comeback Dressing
Cost $5
Prep Time 10 minutes

This is just too good. Use on salads or as a dipping sauce with chicken strips.

    2 cloves garlic, minced
    1 cup mayonnaise
    2 Tbsp. water
    ¼ cup chili sauce
    ¾ cup ketchup
    1 Tbsp. prepared mustard
    ½ cup oil
    1 Tbsp. Worcestershire Sauce
    1 Tbsp. pepper
    1 small onion, grated

Garlic powder and onion powder can be substituted for garlic and onion. Place ingredients in blender and blend. Store covered in refrigerator for several days before using to allow flavors to blend.

Potato Salad

Cost $4

Prep and Cooking Time 30 minutes, plus time to chill

l

2 eggs
5-6 potatoes or amount needed to feed your
  family, peeled and cut into chunks
¼ cup onion, finely chopped
2 Tbsp. oil
Salt
Pepper
1 Tbsp. prepared mustard, either yellow or Dijon
  Mayonnaise, regular or light, or Miracle Whip
Paprika

This recipe comes from playing in the kitchen and lots of family cookouts and summer holiday gatherings. This is also a nice light lunch.

Put eggs and potatoes in large pot to boil. (A time-saving move, since you want hard-boiled eggs and boiled potatoes!) While eggs and potatoes are boiling, put oil, onion, mustard and salt and pepper to taste into your favorite salad bowl or serving dish.

When potatoes are tender, drain, removing eggs. Remove shells from hard-boiled eggs and slice. Place in salad bowl. Run cold water over potatoes to cool and add them to salad bowl. Add desired amount of mayonnaise to salad bowl and mix lightly to combine all ingredients. Sprinkle with paprika for a flavorful and decorative touch. Refrigerate for several hours before serving. Delicious with grilled or fried chicken or barbecued ribs.

Corn Salad

Cost $7
Prep Time 20 minutes

2 cans whole kernel corn, white or golden, drained
1 large tomato, chopped
1 small onion, finely chopped
6 green onions, chopped
1 small cucumber, peeled and chopped
½ bell pepper, chopped
Mayonnaise
Salt
Pepper

Mix all ingredients in your favorite salad bowl or serving dish, seasoning with salt and pepper to taste and blending with about ¼ cup mayonnaise, more or less depending on preference. Refrigerate until ready to serve. This is also a yummy and colorful side dish with grilled chicken.

Seven-Layer Salad

Cost $12
Prep Time 30 minutes

1 pound bacon, fried, drained and crumbled
1 head Iceberg lettuce, rinsed and torn into
  bite-sized pieces
1 red onion, chopped
1 10-ounce package frozen green peas, thawed
10 ounces cheddar cheese, shredded
cup chopped cauliflower
1¼ cups mayonnaise mixed with 2 Tbsp. sugar
  (or 1 ¼ cups Miracle Whip without sugar mixed in)
2/3 cup Parmesan cheese, grated

If you've got a pretty glass salad bowl or trifle dish, this is what to put in it. Seven-Layer Salad is always a hit at parties, and it pairs up nicely with everything from grilled chicken and steak to meatloaf and pasta dishes.

In salad bowl or serving dish, place lettuce as the first layer, then chopped red onion, peas, shredded cheddar cheese, cauliflower and bacon. Spread top of salad with mayonnaise mixture or Miracle Whip. Top with grated Parmesan cheese. Refrigerate until serving.

Olive Garden Salad

Cost $10
Prep Time 10 minutes

1 bag Iceberg lettuce mix for salad
¼ red onion, sliced very thin into rings
Pitted black olives, to taste
5-6 mild pepperoncini peppers
1 tomato, sliced
½ cup croutons
Italian dressing or vinaigrette (use your favorite brand)
Grated Parmesan cheese
Freshly ground black pepper, to taste

I love the salad at Olive Garden, and one evening, at a girls' night in, the hostess served up something similar. I've done my best to copy hers, because every good recipe is worth stealing.

In your favorite salad bowl or serving dish, toss together salad greens, sliced red onion, olives, peppers, sliced tomato and croutons with Italian dressing or vinaigrette. Top with grated Parmesan cheese and ground black pepper.

At the girls' night, which was also a Pampered Chef party, we had the salad for dinner with freshly baked rolls and pork tenderloin, but this would be wonderful with lasagna or another favorite hearty pasta dish.

Fall Salad
Serves about 4
Cost $8
Prep Time 10 minutes

1 bag spring mix greens
1 green apple (Granny Smith), chopped into bite-sized
  pieces
1 red-skinned apple (Jonathan or Fuji work well),
chopped into bite-sized pieces
½ to 1 cup pecans, pieces or halves
Nonstick cooking spray
Cinnamon sugar
Shredded cheddar cheese
Vinaigrette dressing (your favorite)

Place rinsed greens in your favorite salad bowl. Toss
in apple pieces.

Put pecans on a plate and spray lightly with nonstick
cooking spray and sprinkle with cinnamon sugar.
Microwave for a minute. Sprinkle sugared pecans into
salad. Add cheddar cheese to taste, and toss with your
favorite vinaigrette dressing.

Deviled Eggs

Cost $3

Prep and Cooking Time 30 minutes, plus time to chill

6 eggs
¼ cup mayonnaise
1 tsp. prepared mustard (yellow gives a nice color,
  or add zip with a spicy mustard)
Salt
Pepper
1 tsp. vinegar
1-2 tsp. sweet pickle relish
Paprika

Deviled eggs were something I feared as a child. "Devil" was in the name, after all, and what if you used Hellman's mayonnaise?

You have "Devil" and "Hell" together in one recipe! But these are quite heavenly. We love them so much I even have a Tupperware Deviled Egg keeper, but it's not like these stay around for long! These are yummy with fried chicken or ham, serve them up with a salad lunch.

Hard boil eggs and cool with ice water to prevent a grey ring around yolks. Peel eggs and slice in half lengthwise. Remove yolks and place in bowl. Place egg whites on serving plate.

Mash yolks with mayonnaise, mustard, salt and pepper to taste, vinegar and desired amount of sweet pickle relish. Spoon about a teaspoon of egg yolk mixture into each egg half. Sprinkle with paprika and refrigerate until ready to serve.

Curried Chicken Salad
Cost $10
Prep Time 30 minutes

My sons love chicken salad, and I love using up leftovers. They're usually happy with crackers and a chicken salad made with chicken leftovers mixed with mayonnaise and curry powder, but if you want to kick things up a notch, make this. It's yummy and beautiful served on salad greens. It's enough to make you want to cook extra chicken for planned leftovers.

2 cups cooked chicken, shredded or cubed
¾ cup mayonnaise
2 tsp. lemon juice
¾ tsp. curry powder
1 medium apple, cored and chopped (Granny Smith, Gala or Fuji work well)
¾ cup dried cranberries
½ cup thinly sliced celery
¼ cup chopped pecans
2 Tbsp. chopped green onions

Mix mayonnaise, lemon juice and curry powder. Blend with chicken, apples, dried cranberries, celery, pecans and onions. Refrigerate until serving. Best eaten the same day it is prepared.

Tuna Salad
Cost $3
Prep Time 5 minutes

There is nothing as comforting as Tuna Salad, either on toast or crackers. It's also yummy with tomato soup on a cold day.

1 6-ounce cans light tuna in water
1/3 cup mayonnaise
Lemon juice
Salt
Pepper
1 tsp. sweet pickle relish (optional)

Drain tuna and mix with mayonnaise. Season with a squeeze of lemon juice and salt and pepper to taste. If you like a sweeter tuna salad, mix in pickle relish. Refrigerate until ready to serve.

10

Odds and Ends:
Stuff That Didn't Fit
Anywhere Else

Odds and Ends

There are always things that don't quite fit into neat little categories.

Recipes, for one. Some you can call a casserole, a salad or a dessert, but then there are some things that are wonderful just as they are, but defining them as an odd or an end is probably the way to go.

People are like that, too. We can be hard to define, and some of us, just when you have us figured out, we change.

You just can't pin us down.

It's a good thing, not fitting into molds and expectations. How boring life would be if we did!

Everyone is a little bit of an odd or an end, funnier or deeper or more thoughtful or kinder than you might have thought, and everyone has his or her own style. No two of us are alike.

Each of us, when cooking, interacting, working or playing, has a unique flavor to bring.

While you bring your loved ones together around your table, make sure to bring that special ingredient, your own uniqueness, and stir it in.

Be you, that indefinable you, because you've got more practice being you than anyone else. No one can be you better than you can. Don't settle for being in someone's category. Live life fully, and be so thankful for the blessings of life that you forget about the hardships. Say grace, then experience it.

Maggie and Jiggs

Cost $3
Prep and Bake Time 10 minutes

Back in my high school days, my BFF Melanie
Elmore made this one time at her house when we were
spending an afternoon playing the board game Life. It was
so good I then made this at my house, and I've whipped
these up on the fly ever since. I love the name of this
snack, Maggie and Jiggs, because I used to love reading
the comic strip "Bringing Up Father." Maggie and Jiggs
were the main characters, although this snack is sweeter
than those two ever were. I love the saltiness of the peanut
butter and crackers with the sweet marshmallows.

12 Saltine crackers
Creamy peanut butter
12 large marshmallows

Preheat oven to 400. Spread peanut butter on 12
Saltine crackers and place them in rows on a baking sheet.
Place a marshmallow on top of each cracker. Bake at 400
until marshmallows are toasted and browned. Remove and
cool slightly before serving.

Grandma's Cheap-O Jell-O Parfaits
Serves 4
Cost less than $1
Prep Time 5 minutes, plus time to chill

This is something our sweet Grandma, rest her soul, learned from living through the Great Depression only to go on to live frugally as a kindergarten teacher and graduate student before being a wife and mother. This is best when served up in clear glasses or bowls so the layers show. I loved this as a girl, and my children loved this, too. Lots of wows for less than a dollar, plus this is literally as easy as boiling water.

1 box Jell-O, any flavor
Water

Mix Jell-O according to package directions, but do the mixing in a blender. Pour the hot water and Jell-O mixture in the blender first, then the cold water. Blend for about 1-2 minutes. You should have a frothy batch of Jello and little, if any, of it that is not whitish with bubbles. Pour into serving dishes and refrigerate until firm. The result is a dark layer of Jell-o topped with a frothy but firm layer.

Christmas Crack

Cost $8, with pecans
Prep and Cooking Time 15 minutes

1 sleeve Saltine crackers
1 cup butter
1 cup brown sugar
2 cups chocolate chips
Sprinkles or chopped pecans, if desired

Warning: This stuff is so addictive! I tried this at a party, and it was all I could do to not scarf down the whole tray. This is delicious at Christmastime and makes a great gift. It will keep for up to two weeks in the refrigerator.

Preheat oven to 350. Cover a baking sheet with parchment paper or aluminum foil. Place crackers in a single layer on baking sheet.

Combine brown sugar and butter in a saucepan over medium heat, stirring constantly. Boil for three minutes without stirring and remove from heat.

Pour hot brown sugar-butter syrup over Saltine crackers and bake for 5 minutes.

Remove from oven and quickly sprinkle crackers with chocolate chips. Put back in oven for 1 minute. Remove and use a spatula to spread chocolate over crackers. Add sprinkles or top with chopped pecans if desired.

Place in freezer for an hour, then break apart and serve it up or store for later in a covered container.

Ranch Crackers
Makes 5 cups
Cost $4
Prep and Bake Time 15 minutes

These things are so easy, and they're great to have around during the holidays or football season.

1 envelope Ranch dressing mix
½ tsp. dried dill weed
¼ cup cooking oil
¼ tsp. lemon pepper
¼ tsp. garlic powder
5 cups oyster crackers

Preheat oven to 250. In large bowl, combine Ranch dressing mix, dill weed, cooking oil, lemon pepper and garlic powder. Add oyster crackers and toss to coat.

Spread evenly on a baking sheet and bake for about 15 minutes. Stir after about 7-10 minutes. Allow to cool before serving, and store any leftovers in a covered container or zippered plastic bag.

Fire Crackers
Serves about 30
Cost $6
Prep Time 15 minutes

I know you are thinking that my family and I must eat a lot of crackers for me to have this many ideas for playing with Saltines and such in the kitchen. And you would be right. They're one of my favorite snacks.

1 2/3 cup cooking oil
1 tsp. garlic powder
1 tsp. onion powder
½ tsp. black pepper
2 envelopes Ranch dressing mix
3 Tbsp. crushed red pepper flakes
1 16.5-ounce package of Saltines, regular or multigrain

In a 2-gallon zippered plastic bag, combine cooking oil and seasonings. Add crackers and flip over a few times to get seasonings to all the crackers. Lay flat and let sit an hour. Turn again, making sure crackers are well coated. Let sit overnight. Crackers will be ready to serve in the morning. No baking required! If you only have 1-gallon bags, divide oil, seasonings and crackers between two bags and continue as directed.

Drunk Chicken
Serves 4
Cost $7
Prep and Cooking Time 1 hour

1 chicken, whole
1 tall can of cheap beer, regular or light. You can use
  a 12-ounce can but it is harder to remove.
Seasoned salt or Cajun seasoning
1 sprig rosemary, optional

You've got to love a recipe that requires you to put a tall-boy beer up the back end of a chicken.

Wash chicken and pat dry. Season inside and out with seasoned salt or Cajun seasoning. Start grill, either gas or charcoal.

Drink about ¼ cup of the beer. Or pour it off, but that's less fun.

If you are using rosemary (I have some growing in the garden), put the sprig inside the can.

Put chicken on grill and cook with indirect heat for 1 hour. It will be sitting as if it was standing on its drumsticks. Chicken is done when juices run clear.

Cut into quarters and serve. This is great with Baked Beans and Potato Salad.

Pretzel Turtles
Makes about 12-15 pieces
Cost $8
Prep and Bake Time 15 minutes, plus time to cool

This recipe is a favorite of mine at Christmastime. You get the indulgent flavor of turtle candies, the candy turns out pretty and they are easy to make.

1 large bag Tiny Twist pretzels (these are the little ones)
2 packages Rolos or miniature Milky Way candies
1 bag pecan halves

Preheat oven to 350. Cover a baking sheet with foil for easy clean-up.

Place pretzels out on baking sheet in rows. Place an unwrapped candy on top of each pretzel.

Place in oven. Do not answer the door or the phone. Stand right there, watching the candies. When chocolate turns shiny, which does not take long, immediately remove from oven. Right away, mash a pecan half into candy, smashing it. Cool in freezer about an hour or until chocolate has set. Store in a covered container.

Turkey Soup

Cost $4
Prep and Cooking Time 2 hours

1 turkey frame
Chicken bouillon cubes
Vinegar
1 onion, chopped
1 cup celery, chopped
1 cup carrots, cleaned and sliced
6 ounces or more noodles (your favorite shape)

We may have the turkey and dressing with all the trimmings at Thanksgiving, but this is a coveted round 2. My Dear Sons, when in college, wanted containers of this to take back to their apartments. It comes from years of being a tightwad, stretching our food dollars and feeding a big family. It freezes well and will make your house smell wonderful when simmering.

After you and your family have enjoyed Thanksgiving dinner and you've cleared the table, take most of meat off turkey frame. Take carcass and put in your largest stock pot (you will need two big pots). Fill with water to cover bones. Add 1 Tbsp. vinegar, which you won't taste. It helps pull calcium from the turkey bones, though, so it makes your broth more nutritious.

Cheat to make your broth prettier and tastier by adding 2 or three bouillon cubes to water. Bring to a boil and simmer for about two hours. Do other things while this is going on, such as watch football on TV or pull out the Christmas decorations.

When turkey is completely falling apart, remove carcass from broth and let cool. Take broth and strain through a colander lined with a clean kitchen towel or cheesecloth into another stock pot. This will make your broth clear and pretty.

Refrigerate broth so fat rises to top and can be removed.

Meanwhile, remove meat from carcass and chop into bite-sized pieces. Refrigerate until ready to make soup. Ready? OK, good. Put broth on to boil. Add meat, carrots, onions and celery along with noodles. Simmer until vegetables are tender and noodles are done. If you have leftover peas from Thanksgiving dinner, add them.

Serve this up with leftover rolls from dinner, and you have lunch or supper.

Taco Popcorn
Cost $2
Prep and Cooking Time 3 minutes

1 bag butter flavored microwave popcorn
½ envelope taco seasoning

Pop popcorn and pour into a large serving bowl.
Sprinkle with taco seasoning.

Get creative – the Dear Daughter and I love shaking
some nontraditional seasonings on popcorn. Try lemon
pepper, Cajun seasoning or Mrs. Dash blends.

Homemade Pizza

Cost $8, depending on ingredients
Prep and Cooking Time about 90 minutes

1 envelope active dry yeast
1 to 1 1/8 cup warm water
1 Tbsp. olive oil
1 cup all-purpose flour
1 ¼ tsp. salt

I feel like something of a traitor since one of my sons worked making and delivering pizza most of high school and all of college; but takeout pizza has its place, on nights when life gets the better of you. It is like manna from heaven when you have no idea how dinner will get on the table. Homemade pizza is something you take a little time with and enjoy. Making one can become a family activity, and trust me, kids love dotting the family pizza with slices of pepperoni, sausage and veggies.

Dissolve yeast in 2 Tbsp. warm water. Once yeast is dissolved, mix with all other ingredients, using hands or a mixer, until dough is soft and smooth. Knead, but dough should still have a rough outward texture. Place dough in a greased bowl and cover, allowing to rise in a warm place for about an hour. This should be enough dough for two 14-inch pizzas.

For the sauce, simmer a small can of tomato sauce with 1 tsp. sugar, ¼ cup red wine (optional) and 1 tsp. of Italian seasoning for about 10 minutes.

To make pizzas, shape dough into a crust. Ours never have been pretty, but as they say in north Mississippi, they still "eat good." Allow dough to rest 15 minutes after shaping.

Preheat oven to 450 and bake pizza crust for about 8 minutes.

Remove and top: Spread sauce on pizza to taste, saving any left over to use as a dipping sauce. You can also freeze this for use in stews or in making spaghetti sauce.

Top pizzas with your favorite toppings: sliced pepperoni and mushrooms, chopped onions and bell peppers, sausage and black olives. Make them like you like them.

Top with shredded mozzarella cheese, or use your favorite blend of shredded cheeses.

Bake for about 10 minutes to melt cheese and brown crust, keeping a close eye on them. If you used the wine in the sauce, then pour yourself a glass and enjoy your pizza with a fresh green salad.

Spiced Tea Mix
Cost $5

Prep Time 5 minutes

Back in the 1970s, this was the rage. Everyone was drinking this stuff, especially during the holidays. You'd even go to teas and there it would be, a coffee urn dedicated to spiced tea. It's still yummy, by the way, and it also is a sweet gift when bagged up with a coffee mug for teachers, Sunday school leaders and the like.

2 cups Tang
½ cup instant tea
1 ½ cup sugar
1 large envelope lemonade mix
1 Tbsp. ground cloves
1 tsp. cinnamon

Mix all ingredients and store in an air-tight container.

Beer Bread
Makes 12 muffins
Cost$3
Prep and Bake Time 30 minutes

If you are trying to disguise leftovers as another meal and want to kick it up a notch, this is something quick and easy to add. A basket of fresh-baked bread makes it look like you made an effort, and the beer in this gives a nice yeasty flavor. If you want to only make six muffins, fine, but you have to then drink ¾ of a can of beer.

2 cups Bisquick
2 Tbsp. sugar

Preheat oven to 450. Drink ½ can of beer. Spray muffin pan with nonstick cooking spray.

In large mixing bowl, stir together the other ½ can of beer, Bisquick and sugar. Spoon batter into muffin pan and bake at 450 for about 10-15 minutes or until done.

Cupid's Crackers

Cost $6
Prep Time 30 minutes

Ritz crackers
Peanut butter
White chocolate candy coating
Red and pink sprinkles

This is something my mama would whip up as Valentine's Day treats. My playing with crackers in the kitchen comes honest.

Make sandwiches with Ritz crackers and peanut butter. Melt white chocolate candy coating according to package directions. Dip cracker sandwiches into candy coating and place on a foil-lined baking sheet. Immediately decorate with sprinkles. Refrigerate until set. You can use this for other holidays by changing the color of the sprinkles.

Butterscotch Haystacks

Cost $5
Prep Time 15 minutes

1 bag butterscotch chips
1 small can Chow Mein noodles
1 cup peanuts

Another of my mama's favorites.

Melt butterscotch pieces. Stir in noodles and peanuts. Drop by teaspoonfuls onto a foil-lined baking sheet. Refrigerate until set.

John and Copeland's Baked Green Beans

Cost $3
Prep and Bake 30 minutes

1 ½ pounds fresh green beans
2 Tbsp. extra virgin olive oil
1 tsp. salt
½ tsp. black pepper

My middle son and his sweet girlfriend gave me this recipe, and he even made these for us when on a visit back home. They're so delicious they're addictive.

Preheat oven to 400. Wash green beans and pat dry with paper towels, trimming off any stems. Add to large mixing bowl. Coat green beans with extra virgin olive oil.

Cover baking sheet with aluminum foil. Place beans in a layer on foil. Sprinkle green beans with salt and pepper.

Bake for about 20 minutes, turning about 10 minutes into cooking time to make sure green beans are evenly done.

Homemade Play Dough
Cost $3
Prep Time 30 minutes

2 cups all-purpose flour
2 Tbsp. oil
½ cup salt
2 Tbsp. cream of tartar
Up to 1 ½ cups boiling water (Pour gradually to get to
    consistency that looks right to you)
Food coloring

Mix flour, salt, cream of tartar and oil in a large
mixing bowl. Add food coloring and boiling water and stir
until combined. Let it cool, and knead well. If it is still
sticky, add more flour to get consistency right. Store in a
zippered plastic container. This will keep for up to six
months.

Jezebel Sauce
Cost $5
Prep Time 10 minutes

1 10-ounce jar apple jelly
1 10-ounce jar pineapple preserves
1 8-ounce jar horseradish
1 Tbsp. dry mustard
1 tsp. black pepper

This sauce is sweet but hot and spicy, just like you might imagine the Biblical Jezebel being. She was one of the original bad girls of the Bible. In my growing-up years, if you wanted to insult a woman, call her a Jezebel.

Anyhow, the first time I had this sauce, it was with a baked ham, and it is fantastic as a go-along with ham or poured over a block of cream cheese and served with crackers.

In a mixing bowl combine all ingredients until well blended. Store in refrigerator, and let chill overnight before serving so flavors can marry.

Hot Chocolate Mix
Cost $3

Prep Time 5 minutes

This is simple and handy to have on hand. It's a warm and comforting way to start a cold morning. Bag this up or put in Mason jars for a sweet gift for neighbors, Sunday school leaders, teachers and the like.

3 cups nonfat powdered milk
¾ cup sugar
½ cup unsweetened cocoa powder
1/8 tsp. salt
½ tsp. cinnamon (optional – gives the mix the taste
of Mexican chocolate)

For each serving, add ¼ cup mix to 1 cup boiling water in a mug. Don't forget the marshmallows!

Fireside Coffee Mixes
Cost $6
Prep Time 5 minutes

Gourmet coffee can be on the pricey side if you hit the coffee shops. Keep this on hand and you can get your java fix a mug at a time and tuck away the savings. This is also a nice gift when paired up with a coffee mug.

Basic mix
¼ cup instant coffee granules
¼ cup nondairy powdered coffee creamer
1/3 cup sugar

Combine and store in a zippered plastic container. To make by the mug, add 2 Tbsp. mix to a mug of boiling water.

Mocha
Add 2 tsp. unsweetened cocoa powder to mix.

Viennese
Add ½ tsp. to 1 tsp. cinnamon to mix.

ALSO BY THIS AUTHOR

Because I Said So!

Life in the Mom Zone

Annie Oeth